Hythe Pier and Ferry — A History

ISBN 0 9507620 0 8
Printed and published by Itchen Printers Limited, Southampton
First edition June 1981
Second edition April 1986

Contents

Introduction

There has been a ferry of sorts from Hythe since time immemorial. Numerous columnists, diarists and essayists have recorded events for posterity but never has anything comprehensive been successfully undertaken. This attempt to do so doesn't claim to include everything that has happened here, but does claim, so far as the ferry is concerned, not to have missed very much.

Although this is a story about one particular aspect of the village, references to changes and developments in Hythe and district are scattered through the text along with illustrations that show through all these changes, it has lost little of it's charm.

Local histories are full of great characters who in the wider world disappear into inconsequence. Their efforts must not be overlooked and those involved with the Hythe-Southampton Ferry, some even only remotely so, are given attention alongside the more important developments.

So, now, I set out to relate the story of this not unimportant part of local life, which will, I hope, stir an admiration for those long since gone, revive memories of those just so and inspire those of us still here, who probably take the ferry facilities very much for granted, to make tomorrow's history equally interesting.

Sources of reference.

My main source has been contemporary reports and accounts in the various local newspapers, including the Hampshire Advertiser, Hampshire Independent, Southampton times, Southern Daily Echo and Southern Evening Echo, copies of which are held in the Southampton Central Library at the Civic Centre. Considerable information, too, has been drawn from assorted letters, documents, plans, handbills etc. held in the Hampshire Record Office in Winchester and the Civic Record Office at the Southampton Civic Centre. Much, also, has been extracted from anonymous accounts, some of which have come into my possession and others held by certain individuals and societies. One or two snipets of information have been found in assorted copies of the monthly "give-away" Forest and Waterside Observer with Totton Times and the Hampshire Magazine.

Among the numerous books read the following have given direct assistance; "The Story of Southampton Harbour" by E.A. Shillington. "A History of Southampton 1700—1914 Volume 1", by A. Temple Patterson. "History of Southampton" by Dr. Speed, "The Beaulieu Record" by H.E.R. Widnell and various editions of the assortment of Southampton guides and Directories published over the years. Leads have come from assorted other volumes including among them Capt. F.T. O'Brien's "Early Solent Steamers", "Old Southampton Shores" by the late J.P.M. Pannell and the Eltrac publication "The Hythe-Southampton Ferry" by Bert Moody and W.A. Stearn. Minute books of Southampton Harbour Board and Dibden Parish Council meetings have also proved invaluable.

Acknowledgements.

My greatest debt is to the late Commander J.D. Percy, formerly Managing Director and Chairman of the General Estates Company, the proprietors of the Hythe-Southampton Ferry. Commander Percy provided me with every assistance and encouragement and with his wife, Elisabeth, every hospitality when he, myself and my wife met. His brother and successor, Mr. T.M. Percy , and general manager, Mr. R.R.J. Morgan are also afforded my most sincere thanks. My thanks also go to the staff of the Central Library, Southampton, the Civic Record Office, Southampton, the Hampshire Record Office in Winchester, the Southampton University Library, the British Transport Docks Board at Southampton and the Fawley Local History Group. Several individuals must be mentioned at this point, including Mrs. Jean Sizer, Clerk of the Dibden Parish Council, Mr. W.A. Stearn of the Southern Counties Railway Society, Mr. J.C. Cooper of Messrs. Brazier & Son Ltd., Southampton, Commander John W. Rayner of Southampton, Mr. B.F. Bridges of Bishop's Stortford, Mr. Tony Pritchard of Southampton & District Postcard Collectors Club, Mr. J.H. Pain, Mr. B. Mudge, the late Mr. Len Pearce of Dibden Purlieu, Mr. Harry Banks of Hythe, Miss J.L. Percy and finally, last but not least, my wife, Janet for typing and preparing my manuscript.

Much has happened to the Hythe-Southampton ferry passage since this history was first published in June 1981. This edition not only brings the story up to date but includes several replacement photographs some of which are hitherto unpublished.

Alan Titheridge
Hythe, May 1986

Hotspur IV at Pier pontoon with Queen Mary passing, 1966. (Ronald G. Longman).

In Ancient Times

Saxton's 1575 map of Hampshire carries the entry "Hitheferye", which is the earliest reference to a ferry here and shows that as long ago as early Elizabethan days it was appreciated the shortest route between Hythe and Southampton was there to be used. However, the boatmen of Hythe had been earning their daily bread for many centuries previous and indeed up until comparitively recent times ferrying all kinds of cargo as well as their passengers in and out of the locality.

As were others of his profession residing in and conducting their affairs from Hythe, parts of which belonged to the Honour of Wallingford, boatman and merchant Willelmo (William) Vincort, who is known to have been operating his craft during the year 1440, was exempt from local custom duties. This concession became established as the Honour at this time was in the hands of the Crown, and was to be the reason for many an argument in the centuries that were to come.

The Hythe boatmen were among those delivering timbers to Southampton in 1571. Business being far from plentiful led several of the boatmen to the wrong side of the law, as was the case of John Holford on March 14, 1583 (/4) when for illegally disposing of a boatload of oysters at Millbrook he was brought before the Southampton Admiralty Court.

Indirectly the boatmen were involved in the Armada campaign of 1588. A payment of 5s 8d was received for transporting the crew, their provisions and their cargo of soldiers aboard Southampton's contribution to the fleet, the 120 ton ship **Angel**, lying at anchor off Southampton. A letter signed by Amyas Preston, lieutenant of the **Ark Royal**, dated July 27, 1588 and addressed to the Mayor of Southampton acknowledges receipt of supplies of gunpowder etc. for use against the Armada delivered to the West Country by John Holford on behalf of Southampton. John Holford had been engaged by the Mayor of Southampton and was paid £3 19s 2d "for his boat, himselfe & his men wth their victuells & charges in going to my Lorde Admirall at 2 severall tymes."

Dr. Speed provides the next few instalments to the story in his "History of Southampton" written about 1770. In an entry for 1613 he writes of the Southampton Corporation once applying for a charter for the ferry, upon which one of King James I's Masters of Requests, Sir Christopher Parkins, sent for information on the matter from them. He was told that the fare had always been fixed by virture of their Admiralty Jurisdiction, that is, for a horse and rider —3d, for a man —1d, for market people —½d, for a cow —3d, for an ox —6d and for 20 sheep —6d. Nothing came of this request and Dr. Speed goes on to note that the ferry had been dropped by the Corporation for many years. Later in the book it is remarked that this horse-ferry was lost by neglect.

The ferry continued to be operated by the boatmen, who were obliged by an ancient custom to deposit one boat or lighter load of stones against the Southampton Town Walls within the piles every 6 months. Dr. Speed in an entry for 1683 explains that by complying with the order the boatman would be exempt from paying a toll of 4d each time he landed either passengers or goods. This practise was being neglected so in 1634 an order was made to this effect. These stones protected the Town Walls, when piled along the bottom, from the tides and when filled were known as banks. When repair was needed an order would be made, as in 1609 "The bank under Arundel Tower is order'd to be speedily amended."

During the Civil War, in September 1642, the forces of Parliament took possession of all the boats at Hythe during their advance on and prior to their demand for the surrender of Southampton, which had remained loyal to the King.

View of Southampton from Hythe.

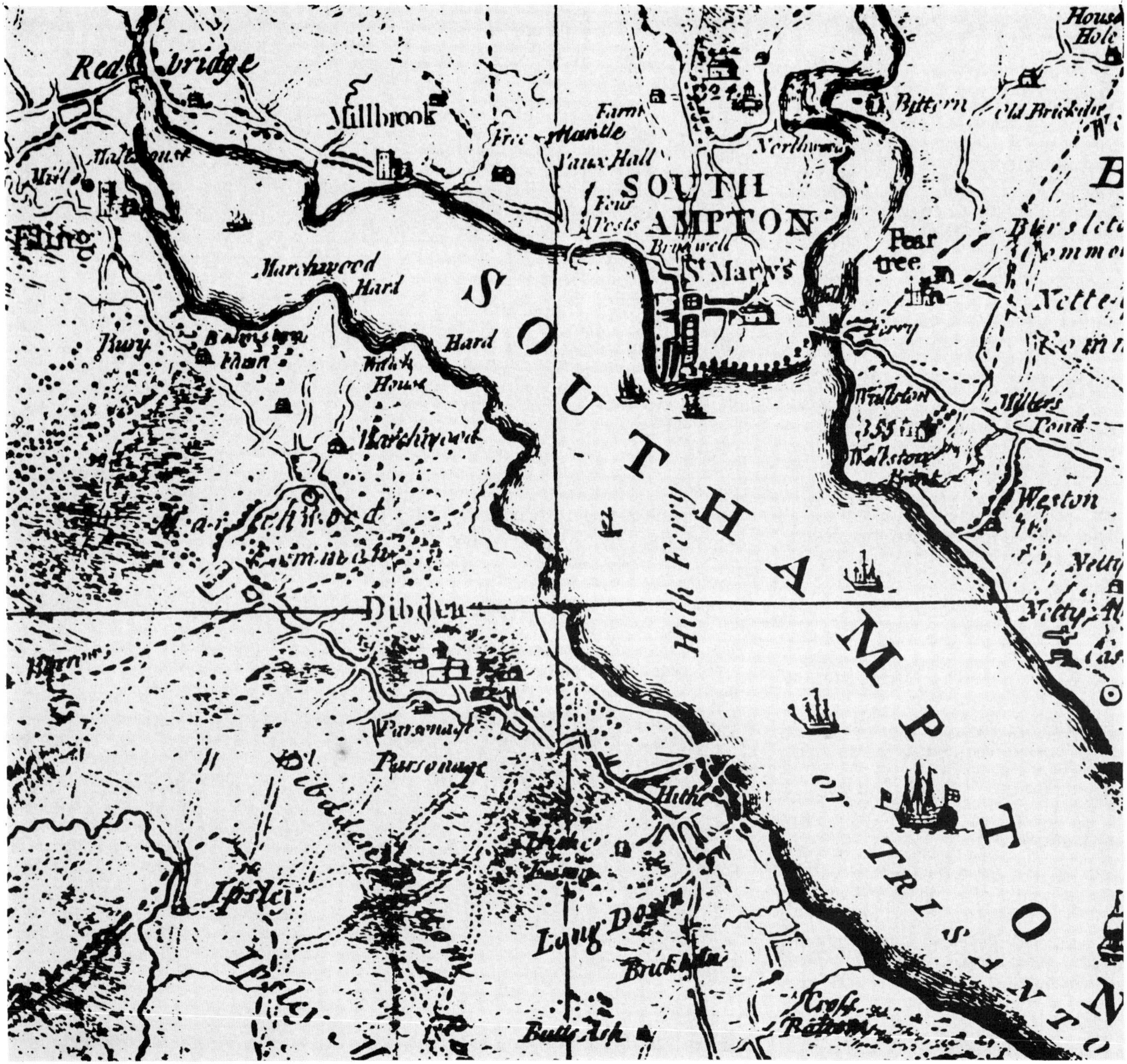

1759 Isaac Taylor Map of Hampshire carrying the entry "Hith Ferry".

The ancient hard at Hythe is widely thought to have been the Deadham Hard in Lucas Malet's (Mary St. Ledger Harrison) romantic novel of the same name, first published on September 11, 1919. The text describes the late eighteenth century hard and shore as a beautiful place.

> "Damaris pointed across the tide-way to the river frontage, including with one sweeping gesture the whole demesne of the Hard from the deep lane on the one hand, opening funnel like upon the shore, past sea-wall-topped at the corner by pink plumed tamarisk, the small twin cannons and pyramid of ball — the lawn and irregular white house overlooking it, backed and flanked by rich growth of trees, to a strip of sandy warren and pine scrub on the other, from out which a line of some half-dozen purple stemmed, red branch Scotch firs, along with the grey stone built Inn and tarred wooden cottages on the promontary beyond, showed through a dancing shimmer of heat haze, against the land-locked, blue and silver waters of Marychurch."

> "The Hard, just now, showed a remarkably engaging countenance, the year standing on the threshold of May. — Mild softly bright weather made amends for a wet and windy April, with sunshine and high forget-me-not blue skies shading to silver along the sea-line. The flower beds, before the garden house-front, were crowded with early tulips, scarlet, golden and shell pink. Shrubberies glowed with rhododendrons, flamed with azaleas. At the corner of the battery and sea-wall, misty grey-green plumes of tamarisk veiled the tender background of grey-blue water and yellow-grey sand."

The ferry was a heavy, flat bottomed, square sterned boat propelled by the boat-man's strength and skill with the oar. He would charge the legal fare of 2d for his services.

As the eighteenth century drew to it's close the potential of Southampton as a great sea-port was beginning to be realised with much improved road communications being made and local groups urging a re-organisation of the administration within the port. The latter materialised, with the passing of the Southampton Harbour Act on April 7, 1803. The Act placed the administration of the Port with a group of Commissioners under the Mayoralty. Early meetings had very little bearing on the ferry, but throughout history the newly formed Board were to be very much involved in all that was to transpire.

A second Act was passed in 1810 to over-come the problems that had arisen from the first. However, it still could not prevent legal disputes in 1822 and 1823. At this time the Commissioners leased out the collection of dues to the highest bidder, whose living was the difference between the offer plus his costs and the actual dues collected. An offer of £750 secured a 3 year lease for Mr. William Hibbs in December 1821. Early in the following year the Commissioners were told of their counsel's opinion that their instruction to the wharfinger on July 23, 1804 "to receive for all small packages and parcels, boxes and trunks intended to be carried to the Isle of Wight the sum of one penny for each package, parcel, box and trunk" was in order despite contrary legal opinion. This cloud of doubt soon spread across the Hythe traffic.

In June 1822 Mr. William Hibbs received notice of 2 writs contesting the dues demanded upon landing from Hythe. The plaintiffs were Mr. G. Ward following a dispute over dues on his personnal dress and the Earl of Cavan who opposed the 3d paid by his butler on a portmanteau and carpet bag. By February 1823 a further 3 lawsuits were pending.

When heard, Mr. Ward's case went against the Commissioners, with 3d. damages being awarded.

The Earl of Cavan's case was heard during July. Once again the verdict went against the Commissioners, Judge Bayley ruling that Hythe was within the Port. This victory was not only a victory for the Earl (whose home was at Eaglehurst), but a victory for the whole of Hythe and it's neighbourhood. While the victors celebrated, the Commiss-ioners were left to count the costs. The clerk's bill alone reached £400 and with other costs totalling £418 the hearings were nothing short of disaster. The losses didn't simply stop there either. There was the refund of the debited dues and the collection of all future "dues" removed from the income. Perhaps it is as well that Mr. Hibbs's thoughts about the situation appear to have passed unrecorded.

The ferry passengers now had an unpro-hibited usage with their number beginning to show marked signs of an increase. The wherrymen were revelling in the Commiss-ioner's gloom but all the while were keeping an eye on another threat to their livlihood — the increasing success of the steamer services between Southampton and the Isle of Wight following their inaug-eration on July 18, 1820 by the **Prince Coburg**. The possibility that one operator or another might extend his operations to include Hythe was feared by all. That poss-ibility became a reality on March 10, 1830 when a whole new chapter in the history of the Hythe Ferry was opened.

Forty Years of Growth 1830 - 1870

THE EMERALD,

(New Steam-Boat,)

For Southampton and Hythe,

AND

For THE ISLE OF WIGHT,

(WEATHER PERMITTING,)

Until the MEDINA, GEORGE IV. & MALMESBURY, take their Station.

SHE will continue to run as follows, during the Week Days, UNTIL FURTHER NOTICE:—

FROM SOUTHAMPTON.

In the Morning at 7 and 8 o'Clock
In the Afternoon at 2, 3, 4, and 5 o'Clock

FROM HYTHE.

In the Morning at 7½, 8½ o'Clock
In the Afternoon at 2½, 3½, 4½, 5½ o'Clock

SOUTHAMPTON TO COWES.

In the Morning at 9½ o'Clock

COWES TO SOUTHAMPTON.

In the Morning at 11½ o'Clock

ON SUNDAYS.—TO HYTHE.

At 8 o'Clock in the Morning, and 5 in the Afternoon.

FROM HYTHE.

At 8½ o'Clock in the Morning, and 5½ in the Afternoon.

FARES—To and from HYTHE and SOUTHAMPTON, 3*d* in Fore Cabin; 6*d*. in the after Cabin. To and from the ISLE OF WIGHT, 1s. 6d. & 3s. 0d.

Every information may be had by application to JOSEPH CLARK, jun. Steam Packet Agent, 47, High-street, Southampton.

N. B.—Passengers are requested to be punctual, as she is intended to start to a Minute, by the Southampton Custom-House time.

Advertisement, Hampshire Advertiser March 6, 1830.

So there it was. The thought that had plagued the minds of the Hythe wherrymen for so many months, in black and white for all to see.

The Hampshire Advertiser for March 13, 1830 tells that "the Hythe Steamer commenced running on Wednesday," Just one day later than advertised. The first "Hythe Steamer" was the "new steam-boat" **Emerald,** built by John Rubie of Cross House, Itchen during the previous Winter for a new company led by Mr. W.C. Westlake. Mr. Westlake's company was formed expressly to build and operate a steamer on the Hythe — Southampton passage, taking only 24 months to fulfil it's objectives. The only vessel owned by this enterprising concern, the wooden constructed paddle steamer **Emerald,** led a very controversial working career almost all of which was spent on the Southampton — Cowes passage.

After completing her trials in February and entering service a month thereafter, the **Emerald** proved to be very popular with the Hythe traffic but did, however, come in for critisism when would-be passengers found themselves stranded in either Hythe or Southampton or being forced to revert to the sailing wherry while she made her daily run to Cowes. Mr. Westlake did not appear at all concerned with the complaints, using the **Emerald,** under the command of engineer J.B. Humphries, for towage and excursion work whenever it suited him.

The **Emerald** recorded 3 different "firsts" during the first 2 years of her career. Not only was she the first Hythe steamer, she was the first steamer operating hour long excursions on Southampton Water and the first available for towage on Southampton Water and the Beaulieu River.

By 1832 the Hythe passage appears to have been discarded altogether with the would-be passengers now committed to using the wherries. The **Emerald** continued to be operated by Mr. Westlake on the Cowes passage until he sold out, much to the displeasure of Capt. Humphries, to the opposition (the Isle of Wight Steam Navigation Co.) late in 1833 for according to Capt. Humphries £1200. The **Emerald** ended her days disintegrating in the mud at Northam. Newspaper notes in 1841 said about her, she "was often plundered but the late Capt. J.H. Knight (Superintendant of the I.O.W. Steam Navigation Co.) viewed her with such disgust that nothing was done."

In June 1835 the Southampton shipbuilding concern of Day, Summers & Co., announced their intention to build an iron paddle boat for the Hythe passage. They went on to say that they had no desire whatsoever to act as proprietors, offering the vessel for sale on completion. The **Forester** was purchased by Capt. J.H. Knight Snr. and Messrs. Smith & Co. who put "the beautiful new and complete Iron Steam Boat" into operation on July 25, 1836. Under the command of Capt. George R. Mason, the Forester continued the service until the early Winter making, however, the occasional excursion to the Beaulieu River and Lymington.

On February 16, 1837 there was a most regretable accident involving the **Forester** as she lay at her mooring off the Hard at Hythe. James Heath, the **Forester's** 17 years old engineer, had been entertaining his friend, a 22 years old Southampton cabinet maker named Thomas Crocker, on what had been for them a very pleasant Sunday. But by 10.30 p.m. the weather had deteriorated so much that George Mason, who in addition to his role as the vessel's skipper was landlord of the Wheatsheaf Inn at

STEAM COMMUNICATION

BETWEEN SOUTHAMPTON, HYTHE, BEAULIEU, LYMINGTON, THE NEW FOREST, &c.

The Public are respectfully informed, that the beautiful new and complete IRON STEAM BOAT,

FORESTER,

(Of Eight-horse Power, built expressly for the station)

WILL, ON AND AFTER MONDAY, JULY 25th, 1836,

LEAVE

HYTHE FOR SOUTHAMPTON,

Every Morning at Seven o'Clock, and every hour after, till eight in the Evening, and the Royal Pier,

SOUTHAMPTON, FOR HYTHE,

AT HALF-PAST SEVEN,

And EVERY HOUR after, till half-past Eight in the Evening.

The FORESTER is well fitted with Fore and Aft Cabins, and every accommodation required for the passage; and the Proprietors earnestly solicit that patronage and support which they hope will be given to those who commence undertakings *for the better accommodation of the Public.*

FARES:—After Cabin 6d., Fore Cabin 3d., including the charge for Landing and Embarking at the Royal Pier.

Further Particulars may be obtained at the Steam Packet Office, next to the Vine Inn, Southampton, and at the Wheat Sheaf and Rodney Inns, Hythe.

Hythe, suggested that Crocker should spend the night aboard the **Forester** with his friend. It would appear that the steamer served regularly as a dormitory for both James Heath and her 12 years old stoker, Samuel Eastman, who was already aboard.

As their punt came alongside the **Forester,** Heath and Crocker called out to Eastman. Both men started to climb aboard but Crocker's inexperience and anxiety to get aboard tipped the tiny craft and both found their way onto the grunnel. Eastman was quick to put 2 ropes over the side but could only render token assistance as the 2 in the water battled to save themselves.

"I have no strength and Crocker holds me so tight," screamed Heath to the helpless stoker. "I shall be obliged to let go."

Eastman put a plank overboard, but to no avail. Their cries for help went unheard. In a final desperate effort Heath and Eastman managed to touch with both hands but in a state of total exhaustion the wretched fellow spoke his last words, "it's of no use I can do no more, may the Lord have mercy upon me."

The **Forester** again took her station for the following Summer but was treated somewhat comtemptibly by the passenger traffic. On cold or wet days the steamer did acceptable business but on the warm and sunny days at the height of the Summer season it was all so very different. The order of such days, which did not pass unnoticed by the proprietors of the **Forester,** were the more liesurely crossings under the power of oar or sail. Even with the installation of a stove into the cabin trade remained insufficient, so much so that during the following March (1838) the proprietors of the steamer repeated an earlier appeal adding the threat of them quitting unless business improved. The threat appears to have worked for the **Forester** operated the ferry during 1839, but in 1840 the volume of traffic slumped to a new low leaving the owners no alternative to terminating their efforts during August.

A proposed transfer to a station between Exeter and Exmouth did not materialise as in October 1840 the **Forester** was employed in the Southampton Docks area as a tug. By 1844 she was lying in the mud at Crab Niton, Itchen and like the **Emerald** she was often plundered as she lay at the mercy of the elements. During March 1844 2 boys aged 9 and 12 were charged at the Southampton Magistrates Court with stealing copper from her but were released because of the withdrawal of prosecution evidence.

In 1842 the Southampton Harbour Board tabled a motion that the numerous watermen carrying passengers between Hythe and Southampton need no longer be licenced; on the surface a strange motion to have passed. Whatever their reasoning, it did nothing to improve the questionable qualifications of some of the previously "licenced" watermen. It must be recorded that in general the watermen were of good and honest character with their crafts in strong and sound condition but some of the antics of the small minority defied all reasoning.

In 1834 each boat was to have by law the owner's licence number painted on the backboard with details of the passenger capacity. Failure to display this information carried a penalty of 40 shillings. Under no circumstances were more than 10 passengers permitted, with reduced maximum numbers for smaller boats, all subject again to a penalty of 40 shillings.

The Harbour Board's decision made no sense when the fearful accident of Sunday May 10, 1840 is recalled. Six excursionists and a waterman died as a Hythe wherry overturned en route home from the Hamble River.

Against advice from many of his colleagues, Hythe waterman James Welch, himself in an intoxicated state, took a party of a dozen dock labourers on an excursion to Calshot Castle. After 10 quarts of beer had been consumed they reached their destination but promptly put to sea again and made for Hamble, where several hours were spent in 2 public houses. The party left for home at about 4 o'clock in the afternoon. All was going well until one or two of the men became alarmed as the waves occasionally broke into the overcrowded boat. They signalled to the **Medina,** on passage to Cowes, but after she had slowed up the men beckoned her to proceed.

Keeping a watchful eye on the situation, Capt. Summers of the **Medina** saw the boat, whilst endeavouring to tack, fill and capsize. A boat was dispatched and the **Medina** herself put about to assist. Six men were picked up, one of whom was thought to be too weak to be revived but the persistance of his rescuer was rewarded. The waterman, although a very good swimmer, drowned with six of his passengers.

After a 2 year free-for-all licencing was re-introduced as part of the provisos of an Act of Parliament passed on July 19, 1844. The Act entitled "An Act for making a Landing Place at or near Hythe in the Parish of Fawley and extra parochial Places adjoining thereto, in the County of Southampton" set up the Hythe Hard Company with a capital of £4500 (150 shares at £30 each). Mr. A.R. Drummond, the leading shareholder, was largely responsible for getting the Act to Parliament and after it had been given the Royal Assent was the leading figure in getting it's provisos so speedily executed.

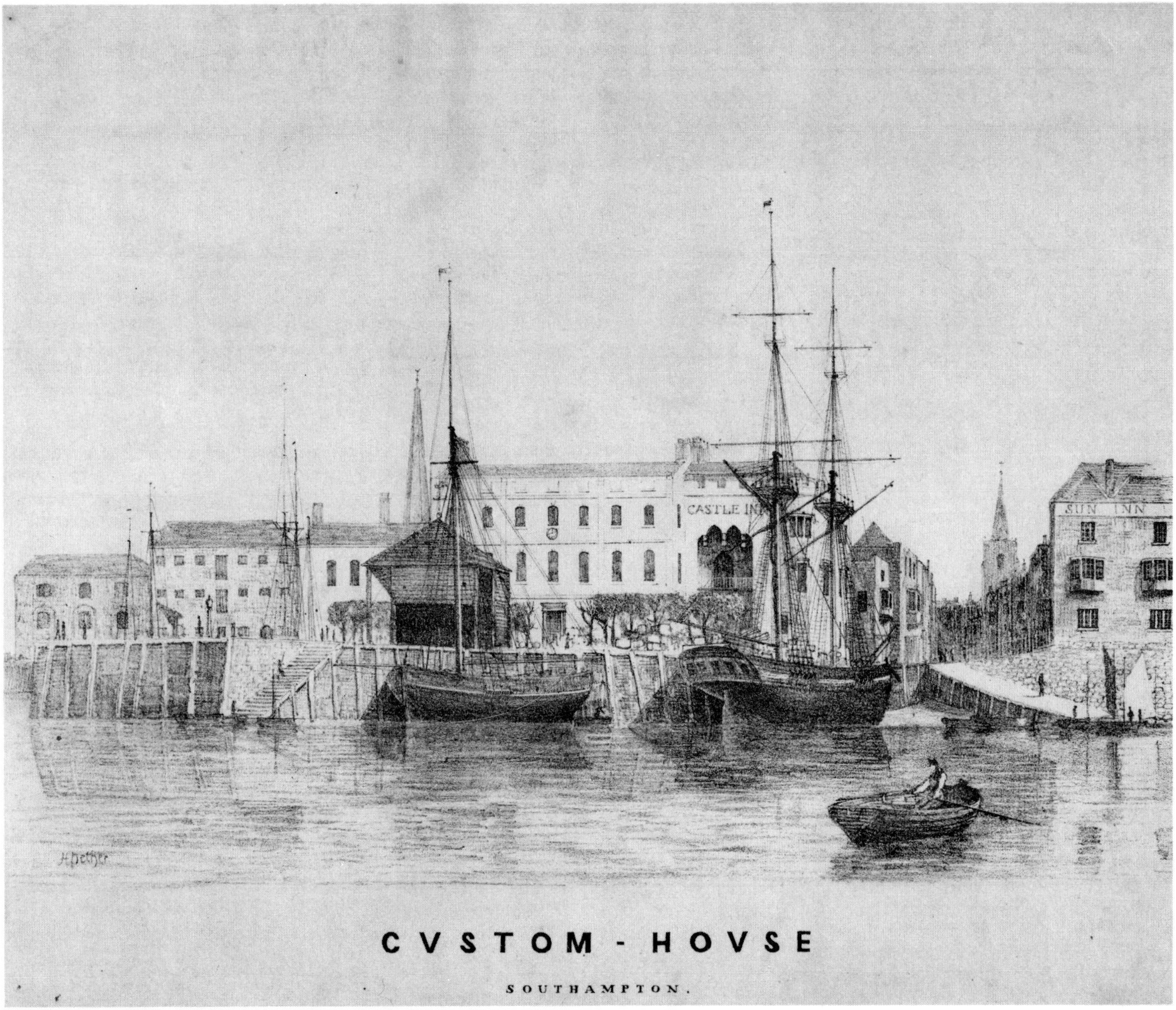

Town Quay area circa 1830.

Mr Andrew Robert Drummond pictured about 1860 (Courtesy Mr Maldwin Drummond J.P. D.L.)

The Hard Company had 10 years in which to construct a new Hard to replace the centuries old and totally inadequate one then in use. Only a little over one of those 10 years was needed as in 1845 the new £7000 stone "pier" was finished and brought into immediate employment.

The watermen, now under licence once again, were obliged to pay a landing fee of 1d for each passenger landed on or within a half mile either side of the Hard. The 1d landing fee was also imposed upon passengers landed from the next steamer on the ferry, the "light and elegant" **Gipsy,** which had entered service on August 25, 1845. Fares were increased by 1d for all fore cabin passengers who crossed the passage after the transfer of operations to the new Hard, much to the annoyance of the patronage whose reactions were that "a halfpenny would have been ample for the mere substitution of stone for gravel."

The **Gipsy** had been built by Messrs. Summers, Day and Baldock at their Northam shipyard and launched on July 5, 1845 by Miss Emily Clarke, daughter of one of the proprietors. After a successful trial run to Beaulieu and Cowes on August 20 she entered service on the Hythe passage under the command of Capt. G.R. Mason, (the same Capt. Mason of the **Forester**), offering an hourly service in each direction.

Like those of the **Emerald** and the **Forester** before them, the proprietors of the **Gipsy** were reduced to calling for better support. The following circular was put about during November 1847 in preparation for a public meeting to call for support scheduled for December 11.

PROPOSED HYTHE STEAM FERRY COMPANY BETWEEN SOUTHAMPTON AND HYTHE

CAPITAL £1280 IN 64 SHARES OF £20 EACH

The convenience of Steam communication to and from the populous neighbourhood of Hythe, so long afforded by the **Gipsy** steamer, is likely to be discontinued, principally from an insufficient local interest and the absence of a second steamer, so essential to success.

The loss of an accommodation once enjoyed, would be felt with increased severity. Influenced by this consideration, and the desire to secure a second steamer, and thereby a constant winter and summer communication, some of the inhabitants of Hythe and neighbourhood have favoured the intention to form a Steam Packet Company.

The necessity of Company would not be required for the amount, but to ensure local interest and a constant and certain communication, which a non-resident propriety might fail to do; and so much confidence have the present owners of the **Gipsy** in the proposed mode of establishing a Steam-Ferry, that they are willing to join in the undertaking, and to take shares to the amount of £320 in the new Company.

In such a Company neither Act of Parliament, nor Deed of Settlement nor any law expenses would be required, the Registration Act (of the Customs) fully protects the owner's property; his shares may be possessed, tranferred, bought or sold, without stamp duty or Solicitor's fees; the division of the shares into sixty-forths meets the necessity of the Custom Laws, and the minutes of proceedings entered into by the proprietors would effectually arrange the details required as to working the boats, keeping the accounts, & c.

It is suggested that all receipts be paid weekly to the Bankers, and a notice published that the debts of the Company are payable monthly, which would effectually free the proprietors from all debts or liabilities, and the mode of accounts and working, as adopted by the **Gipsy's** proprietors, and checking the income and expenditure, in both simple and inexpensive.

From an interview had with the Hythe Hard Company, it has been ascertained that much mutual advantage would result from a reduction in the fore cabin tolls, so as to enable the bulk of the passengers to pass to Southampton and back, both tolls inclusive, for sixpence.

By the present imperfect communication, Ninety Thousand passengers annually cross the Ferry, of which number about a third only have availed themselves of the **Gipsy** and this arising doubtless, from the insufficient number of trips than can be made with one steamer, and the absence of local interest.

It has been ascertained, by a careful calculation, that this small number barely pays; that 60,000 passengers would pay a good return on the proposed investment in two steamers, and the undoubted increase upon that number would form a highly remunerative return.

The following estimate of Income and Expenditure is submitted:— for two boats in the summer and one in the winter.

EARNINGS PER WEEK

	£	s	d
200 Double journies 1st class tickets, at 9d	7	10	0
200 Double journies 2nd class tickets, at 6d	5	0	0
200 Single journies 2nd class tickets, at 4d	3	6	8
200 Single journies 1st class tickets, at 6d	5	0	0
Parcels, Luggage, Dogs, & c	0	10	0
	£21	6	8

WEEKLY WORKING EXPENSES

	£	s	d
Wages	5	15	0
Coals	6	10	0
Engine Stores	0	13	0
Tolls	3	15	0
Sundries	1	0	0
Deterioration, 10 per cent on £1280	2	9	3
	£20	2	3
Net Profit	1	4	5

Equal to 5 per cent dividends

Thus even on this moderate calculation a good interest may be secured for the money invested, and the constant whole ninety thousand passengers now passing may be carried, giving a far more considerable profit, and a valuable Ferry effectually established for the benefit of the proprietors and public.

Applications for shares to be made (on or before 14th November) to Mr. J.R. Stebbing, Optician, 47, High-Street, Southampton or Mr. Winckworth, Toll House, Hythe. November 4, 1847.

The meeting took place on December 11 as planned but was very poorly attended. Very little enthusiasm could be raised among those who did attend and so it was decided to cancel all operations there and then.

It was not until April 1855 that another effort was made to establish a paying steamer service on the ferry. The Hythe and Southampton Steam Ferry Company was incorporated on July 17, 1855 with a capital of £2,500 (500 shares at £5 each). Mr. A.R. Drummond and the Duke of Buccleuch were the leading shareholders.

Mr. Thomas Goater, the company secretary, announced in the same month details of an order placed with a Bristol company for 2 screw steamers but this order was to fall through. Another order was placed therefore, but it was for a paddler from the Northam shipyard of Messrs. Day, Summers & Co. Delivery of this vessel was prolonged for a considerable length of time because of a strike and so the company found it necessary to purchase the Thames paddle steamer **Prince Alfred** as a temporary measure. The 10 years old wooden hulled **Prince Alfred** made a trial run to Beaulieu on February 26, 1856 before taking her station.

The **Prince Alfred** was better received than the **Emerald**, **Forester** and **Gipsy** had been. She met with the approval of the contemporary press, too, the Hampshire Independent (June 7, 1856) saying of her,

> "The **Prince Alfred** steam-boat has been plying for some months between Southampton and Hythe, and is found to be a great accommodation to the inhabitants of the neighbourhood".

The report went on to say that, "the annoyances of former days are passed away, and that Hythe is getting as civil and obliging as could be desired."

Despite these encouraging comments the **Prince Alfred** was not the easiest of vessels to operate. Being of traditional form, she had to be turned about by means of long poles after each crossing in preparation for the return leg. However, she didn't have much time left in the hands of her proprietors as their steamer was due to be launched in December of that year.

Lady Elizabeth Drummond pictured in 1829
(Courtesy Mr Maldwin Drummond)

The launch of this steamer took place as planned in December 1856 and afterwards she was taken to Hythe where all of the local schoolchildren were led out onto the Hard to witness the christening. Lady Elizabeth Drummond performed the ceremony, perpetuating her own name in that of the vessel, **Lady Elizabeth.**

The ferry company, who had by this time added the word "Limited" to it's title and increased it's capital to £5000 (January 6, 1857), sold the **Prince Alfred** to Mr. N. Harvey of Fawley on January 29, 1857. Mr. Harvey continued to operate her alongside the **Lady Elizabeth**.

Although a little better supported than the 3 previous concerns, the ferry company found life tough going. Their problems were increased by the **Lady Elizabeth** which was proving to be "too big for the job." She was a double ended vessel thus not having the problem of the **Prince Alfred** but she could not get near enough to the Hard. Passengers had to be ferried in a boat both at Hythe and Southampton, often getting their feet wet at the least for their troubles. By pick-a-backing willing persons, the watermen were able to offer a dry journey.

In December 1858 the ferry company took delivery of a smaller and more practical new steamer. Four months after disposing of the **Lady Elizabeth,** the dedicated owners of the new vessel, named **Louisa,** were able to try again to fulfil their objectives — the much sought after paying service on the Hythe passage. Like the **Lady Elizabeth** before her, the **Louisa** was a double ended ferry but unlike her predecessor the **Louisa** was able to reach the Hard. She also had an additional rudder which added to her already superior manoeuvrability.

The **Louisa** continued to ply the passage but her owners were finding business as difficult as their predecessors, so it was decided during 1860 that a second steamer linking up with the **Louisa** offering a continuous and unbeatable service would be the answer to their problems. A general meeting was called at noon on January 14, 1861 "for the purpose of obtaining the authority of the shareholders for raising the sum of £1,500 in preference shares at the rate of 6 per cent for the purchase of a new steamboat." Presumably the shareholders had no more faith in a service operated by 2 boats than a service operated by one as by September of the same year the company had gone into liquidation. On September 21 the **Louisa** was sold to Mr. W. Winckworth of Hythe who, incidently, had purchased the **Prince Alfred** as a wreck for demolition only 9 days previous. The company was finally disolved on November 9.

Unlike the shareholders, Mr. Winckworth, the secretary of the Hythe and Southampton Steam Ferry Company at the time of it's dissolution, obviously saw a future for a service with a second steamer as by February 1863 he was able to introduce "his own" second steamer, the **Frederica.** Slightly smaller than the **Louisa**, she was built at the Northam yard of Day, Summers & Company and was joint owned between Mr. Winckworth and a Mr. R. Barns also of Hythe. Mr. Barn's interest terminated on January 22, 1868 when Mr. Winckworth acquired the rights of sole-ownership.

Over the next few years, Mr. Winckworth became the first to make the Hythe passage pay. Part of his success was to him being a good PR man. Often he would lay on an extra boat for the simplest of requests. One such instant was the anniversary celebrations of the Sabbath School of the Independent Chapel in Hythe held during the second week of August 1863. The numbers of the Southampton based guests were few but the provision of the additional boats only added to the good reputation being built by Mr. Winckworth.

The success achieved by Mr. Winckworth meant success for the Hard Company too. The returns (summary) for March 1865, being a typical month.

Ave. no. of Persons daily	186
Ave. Receipts daily (including Persons, Luggage, Sheep, etc.)	18s.
Total no. of Persons for Month	5745
, by Steamer	4963
, by Wherry	782

While by the late 1860's the volume of traffic had increased, the conditions prevailing at Hythe had deteriorated. "It was a common experience to have to wait for the tide to go down, or else wade through the water, to get to the steamer". "At low water, spring tides you not only had the whole of the Hard to walk down but often the steamer could not get alongside, and passengers and luggage had to be carried backwards and forwards in a boat." Something just had to be done.

During 1870 a Bill was put through Parliament for the construction of a pier to replace the existing Hard. The period leading up to the actual construction of the Pier is, however, another story.

Form No. 10 A.

STEAMER.

BILL OF SALE.

Official Number of Ship 22538 **Name of Ship** Louisa

Port Number.... 5 in 1859	Port of Registry.... Southampton	British or Foreign built.... British	How propelled.... Paddles and Steam	Where built.... At Cross House in the Town and County of the Town of Southampton	When built.... 26th December 1858

Number of Decks .. .. one	Build .. .. .. Iron Clinch	Measurements......	Length from the forepart of the Stem under the Bowsprit to the aft side of the head of the stern-post 79 Feet 8 Tenths.	
Number of Masts .. .. one	Galleries .. .. .. Nil		Main breadth to outside of plank 12 Feet 4 Tenths.	
Rigged.. .. .. .. Nil	Head .. .. Nil		Depth in hold from Tonnage Deck to Ceiling at Midships 5 Feet 6 Tenths	
Stern .. .. Round	Framework .. .. .. Iron			

Tonnage.	No. of Tons.
Tonnage under Deck	36.76
Closed in Spaces above the Tonnage Deck, if any; viz.: Space or Spaces between Decks ..	/
Poop	
Round-house	
Other inclosed Spaces (if any), naming them	
Deduct allowance for propelling Power 37/100 ..	13.60
Register Tonnage	23.16

	Tons.
Deduction for Space required for propelling Power .. .. .. 37/100 ..	13.60
Length of Engine Room (if measured) 18 Feet 4 Tenths.	
Number of Engines	Two
Combined Power (estimated Horse Power)	Twenty

I William Winckworth of Hythe in the county of Southampton Gentleman W.W.

in consideration of the Sum of Five Hundred Pounds paid to † me by Frederick Fry of Brightville Hythe in the County of Southampton the Receipt whereof is hereby acknowledged, transfer Sixty four Sixty fourths Shares in the Ship above particularly described, and in her boats, guns, ammunition, small arms, and appurtenances, to the said Frederick Fry

Further ‡ I the said William Winckworth for § myself and my heirs covenant with the said Frederick Fry and ‖ his assigns, that ¶ I have power to transfer in manner aforesaid the premises herein-before expressed to be transferred, and that the same are free from incumbrances **

In witness whereof I have hereunto subscribed my name and affixed my seal this 24th day of May One thousand eight hundred and Seventy two

Executed by the above-named William Winckworth
in the presence of
Alfred Haddon

William Winckworth

Bill of Sale transferring Louisa from William Winkworth to Frederick Fry, May 24, 1872.

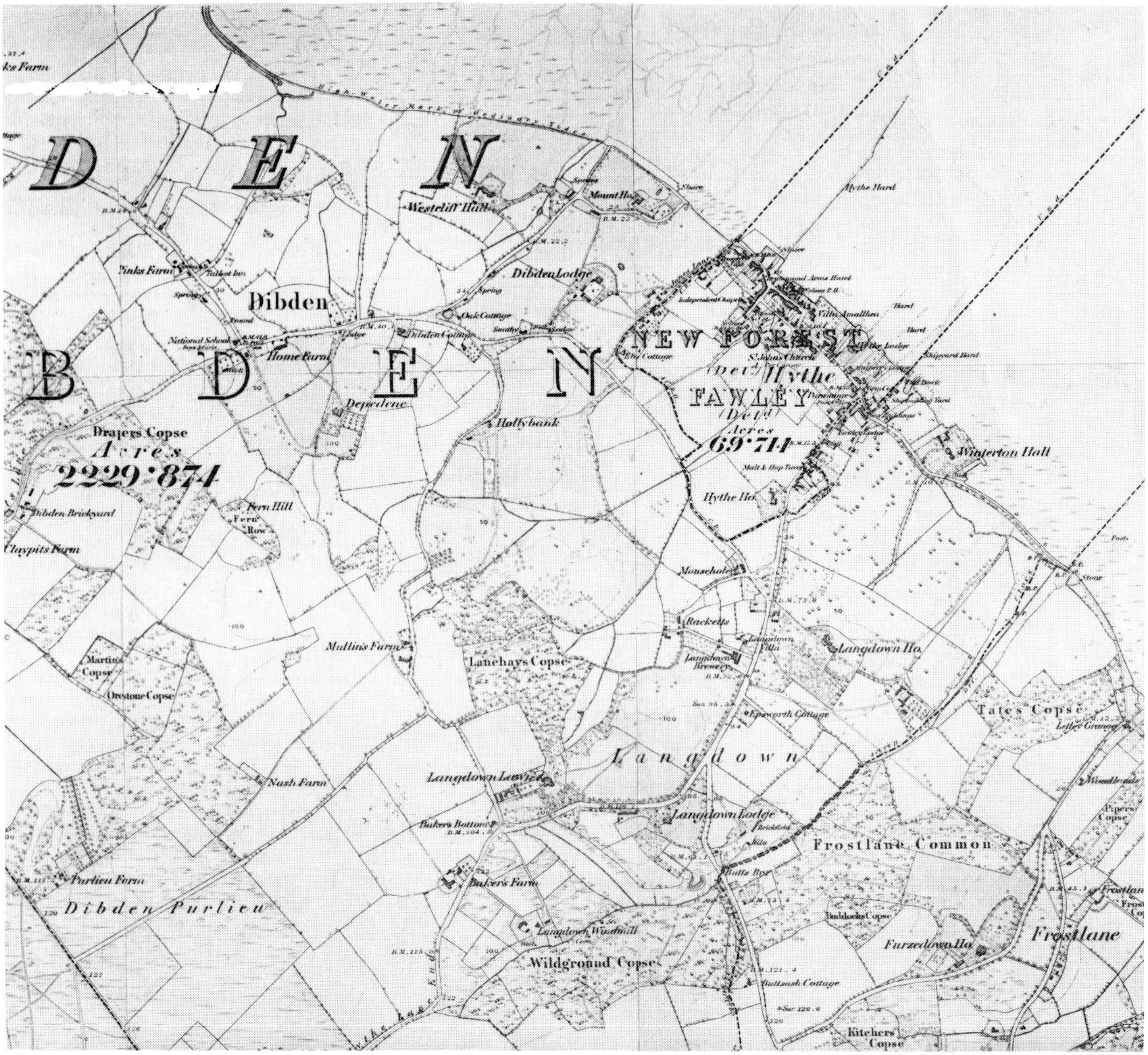

1869 Ordnance Survey Map (Reproduced by permission of the Hampshire County Record Office).

To be or not to be the problem of the 1870's.

Plans for a pier were deposited in the Office of the Clerk of the Peace for Southampton on November 30, 1870.

The plans were for a pier of 2000 feet in length with quite a handsome tollhouse at the shore end and an impressive looking landing pontoon at the seaward end. The landing pontoon with it's method of combating the 13 feet difference between high and low water looked to be the most interesting part of the proposed project. It would appear that there was to be a lifting bridge connecting the end of the pier to the landing pontoon which was the shore end part of a further fixed structure, all parallel to the length of the pier. The bridge was to be a simple construction, semi-circular in profile with girders to the footway, hinged at the shore and on rollers at the seaward ends. It met the pontoon at the centre thus allowing passengers to board or land from the ferries on either side. The landing pontoon would have been raised or lowered, according to the state of the tide, by means of 2 steam pistons, presumably this was the "steam bridge" referred to later. There was also a railway track along the centre of the deck. Messrs. Renshaw and Rolph of 117, Cannon Street, London E.C. had applied for the first Hythe Pier Order.

The subject of the Hythe and Southampton Pier and Steam Ferry Provisional Order, at the time in its' final Parliamentary stages, came in for much consideration by the Southampton Harbour & Pier Board during the early months of 1871. Concern was expressed over one or two clauses in the Order, particularly those wich gave the promotors the final decision as regards the numbers and positioning of all bouys and moorings in the vicinity of the proposed pier and the right to levy a 6d landing toll. Following negotiations, assurances from the Hythe and Southampton Pier and Steam Ferry Company Limited (registered February 1, 1871) were accepted that only sufficient moorings and bouys for vessels using the pier would be laid down and that in general the existing Hythe Hard tolls would be adopted, thus the 6d toll would be forfeited.

The successful conclusion of these negotiations enabled the company to press on with the business of raising the £25,000 authorised capital, a task which had to be performed with some urgency as the powers of the Order were to lapse if work had not started within 2 years.

Local offices were taken, but only £35 of the necessary capital was eventually paid up. Evidence that the Hythe and Southampton Pier and Steam Ferry Company was struggling is to be found in a letter from local representative Mr. Thomas Goater to Mr. A.G. Renshaw (London).

Southampton

May 17th/72

Hythe Pier

Dear Sir,

It was useless to convene a meeting as proposed till replies to the queries submitted had been received and after this receipt the time was insufficient for Saturday. The meeting is therefore indefinitely postponed.

Please inform me if the Company's powers "to go to deep water at low tide" clearly and unquestionably is to go to deep water or low water of Spring tides — also if any negotiation has been opened with the Pier and Harbour Commissioners to pontoon Town Quay (also lengthened) as per 274 — also if as by the printed prospectus it is stated that contract & c may be seen either at your or Messrs. Coxwell's offices you could forward me your copy for the use of meeting if enquired for, but what strikes me as likely to render any meeting nugatory for all practicl purposes is the large sum £11,000* out of £19,000 required.

*Contract price	£22,000
Deduction of Steam Bridge	£3,000
	£19,000

for payment to the Contractors — unless the promoters are prepared to raise at least half this amount outside the district or the Contractors are prepared to accept a much larger payment in Shares. I feel myself confident that the Scheme will fall through for want of subscriptions, I should like to hear anything you may have to remark on this.

I would also suggest that the deduction of £3,000 from the original contract price (£22,000 being the full capital according to the prospectus) for the abandonment of the steam bridge scheme seems scarcely commensurate with the assumed anticipted addition on acct. of such scheme.

So the amount of the deduction open to further consideration so as to increase or diminish the required capital.

Yours truly

signed Thos. Goater

A.G. Renshaw Esq.

April 27.

The 2 year period passed taking the company's powers with it. Hopes of a pier at Hythe were fading fast with the passing of 1873 but at the end of 1874 further interest was brought about when, on November 30, plans were once again deposited at the Office of the Clerk of the Peace for Southampton. These plans show that the engineer, Mr. Greathead, had something in mind that was a lot simpler than his 1870 counterpart. This pier was to be built on cast iron piling on the same site as previously proposed.

Lord Henry Scott pictured by Hythe artist James Kimber

A new company was formed on December 15, 1874 with the somewhat lengthy title of the Hythe Pier and Hythe and Southampton Ferry Company Ltd. to apply for the 1875 Hythe Pier Order, the requirements of which were very similar to that of 1871. The aims of this new and locally supported company included the construction of a pier, the acquisition of Mr. Fry's steamboats (acquired from William Winckworth on May 24, 1872) and the taking over of the Hythe Hard Company's interests. Included among its directors were Messrs. E.A. Drummond of Cadland, R.H. Hobart of Langdown and Lord Henry Scott of Beaulieu — all distinguished local landowners.

Once again the Southampton Harbour & Pier Board raised objections to certain clauses in the (1875) Order but unlike those regarding the earlier Order, this time negotiations became protracted.

Again the 2 year deadline passed and for the people of Hythe so did much of the hope they had in the project. The company, however, were still very much alive and on November 30, 1877 further plans were deposited at the Office of the Clerk of the Peace for Southampton. The plans differed very little from those submitted 3 years earlier, the most obvious alteration being that the first 500 feet was now being shown as a solid construction with the remainder of it's 2000 feet in 45 spans of 33 feet. The company now had to set about raising the necessary funds for the proposed 1878 Hythe Pier Order.

In a meeting of the Southampton Harbour Board, (this shortened title had by this time been adopted), on January 15, 1878 the members were informed that a print of the Provisional Hythe Pier Order, 1878, had been submitted and there was nothing to which the Harbour Board could complain in the Order.

The Royal Assent was given to the Order on July 4, 1878 but not until after Lord Henry Scott, M.P. had used his influence in the House of Commons to obtain an Act with difficulties concerning the Hard Company smoothed away. Now, the Company had everything in their favour, including an Order under very favourable terms and most important, interested sponsors.

A public meeting was held at the Drummond Arms Hotel on February 6, 1879 for the purpose of considering the current position of the project and the methods available to raise the necessary capital. Mr. F.H. Candy (Solicitor) opened

Mr E. A. Drummond (Courtesy Mr Maldwin Drummond)

the proceedings by detailing those present of the failings of the company in complying with its motives following formation in 1874. He went on to say that since the dropping of the 1875 Order, the company had been re-constituted and in the place of the original Board of Directors there were now only 2, Mr. E.A. Drummond and Lord Henry Scott. A Mr. J. Wright now held the position of engineer, and it was he who had found a client prepared to advance the money, but there was the problem with the Hard Company which was eventually solved when the Royal Assent was given to the 1878 Order. The Hard Company had agreed to take payment in ordinary shares in the new Pier Company in lieu of cash as the purchase money. Four hundred and fifty shares of £10 were to be allotted to them. The scheme, for which the original estimate was £8,800, was to raise the level of the shore end of the Hard and to construct a light iron pier with waiting rooms and convenient landing places. This cost could be, in the eyes of Mr. Wright reduced, so he applied to the distinguished engineer Mr. John Dixon, for assistance.

Mr. Dixon agreed to construct a pier with the tramway approaches and waiting rooms for £7,000. As the current markets for iron and labour were very favourable for a work of this kind, he urged the sum be raised quickly. To get this under way, Mr. Dixon had promised to take £1,000 in shares.

Promises to take up the remaining shares flowed liberally before the meeting was concluded in an air of high optimism. By late June all were spoken for, with several persons disappointed.

In their meeting on July 15, 1879 the Southampton Harbour Board heard the reading of a letter from Messrs. Perkins and Candy (Solicitors to the company) informing them that the capital had been raised to build the pier and that a contractor from London, Messrs. Bergheim & Co., had been engaged. The letter also requested improved facilities at the Southampton terminal.

A report in the Southampton Times dated October 11, 1879 told of the arrival at Hythe of the ironwork and that the contractors, who were expected to put a large number of men on the work immediately, had already dug the abutment foundations. Work continued steadily through the winter and in a general meeting held at the Drummond Arms on February 2, 1880, the chairman of the Hythe Pier and Hythe and Southampton Ferry Company was able to give a satisfactory statement both on the progress of the works and of the financial arrangements with the contractors. The necessity of improved facilities at Southampton was discussed before the engineer, Mr. Wright, expressed his faith in the pier being operational by the following May. A further shipment of iron had just been delivered and the remainder, with the timber, was available for transit.

A plan was put forward and adopted for the acquisition of a site for the approach to the pier and the building of a tollhouse and waiting room, in a meeting of the company's shareholders at the Drummond Arms on June 5.

The last pile was driven on June 29 when "flags were displayed in celebration of this accomplishment." Mr. Wright was able to report that all of the piles were fixed and that work could be continued regardless of the weather, to the Directors of the company at their meeting on October 2. The tollhouse and waiting rooms were by this time almost complete so the Directors were able to announce the pier almost ready for public traffic.

The pier met with the approval of the Board of Trade's inspectors in December and was immediately opened to public traffic. An official opening ceremony was arranged for Saturday January 1, 1881 to complete the story of the most important development in the history of the Hythe—Southampton Ferry since Mr. W.C. Westlake introduced his steamer to the passage over 50 years previous.

OATLEY's at the corner of St. John Street and The Marsh in the 1880's.

Hythe Pier during early 1880's with Mr Fry's steamer Frederica and Mr Ted Stevens 60 tons dwt barge George.

One Hundred Years of Hythe Pier 1881 - 1981

Saturday January 1, 1881 was no ordinary New Year's Day. An event held that day realised a dream. The this time that time sometime never promise of a dry landing place for the Hythe ferry traffic had materialised. At 1.00 p.m., accompanied by his entourage, the Mayor of Southampton, left its Royal Pier by steam launch bound for the new Hythe Pier to perform the official opening.

The party was met at the pierhead by Mr. E.A. Drummond, the Chairman of the Hythe Pier and Hythe and Southampton Ferry Company Ltd., and others who had had direct involvement with the project. These included Lord Henry Scott, M.P., (director) and Messrs. F. Fry (owner of the ferry boats and lessee of the pier tolls) and J. Wright C.E. (engineer).

In his speech, the Mayor expressed his delight for the success of the project and hoped that it would draw Hythe and Southampton closer together.
He concluded by declaring the pier open and wishing all present a happy and prosperous new year to a warm round of applause.

Mr. Drummond, in reply, thanked the Mayor for his wishes and his services. Three cheers were then shouted for the Mayor, the company's directors and the Queen before the two official parties retired to the Drummond Arms Hotel for lunch.

Business prospered upon the innovation of the dry landing, first mooted as previous as 1840. The annual total of passengers taken for the company prospectus issued in 1875 was 92,000 but by 1881, (the first year of business completed with the new pier), the figure had arisen to 124,533.

With the motor car, railway and telephone still things of the future Hythe Pier quickly became established as the centre of the community. Everything happening seems to have evolved around the pier, whether it was it's centre or it's starting point. The Hythe Pier Regatta of August 15, 1881 was typical.

After a rainy start, the sun broke through and by mid afternoon the day could be described as being very pleasant. The pier, gaily adorned with national flags and bunting, was surrounded by boats of all shapes and sizes, including the s.s. **Ibis**

Pierhead scene early 1890's.

(owned by H. Bessemer), the s.s. **Una** (E.B. Liebert), the schooner **Reindeer** (Colonel Dugmore), the s.s. **Forest Fly** (Major Foster), the yawls **Brunette** (E.A. Drummond) and **Dove** (Admiral Pearce), the cutters **Hecate** (J.M. Whitchurch), **Dabchick** (R.A. Davies) and **Rosie** (J. Kirby) and the committee vessel Mr. H.G. Stephen's **Spider**. A refreshment bar was provided for the very large crowd who were entertained on the pierhead by the Band of the 1st Hants Volunteer Engineers under the direction of Mr. J.D. Wilson. The steamers did an excellent day's business.

The programme included sailing and rowing events for the Hythe wherrymen. These events took place to the displeasure of their excluded Southampton counterparts.

It is not only Hythe that has been able to reap rewards from the pier. In Southampton, a whole new market was opened up for the neighbourhood of Hythe. For so long the conditions of the old Hard had deterred the Hythe and Beaulieu district farms from buying and selling across the ferry. It was often better for the farmers, particularly those from Beaulieu, to journey to Lymington with the additional mileage doing less damage to animals, property and person than the mud, water and unsafe landing facilities at both the Hard and Southampton Town Quay. The pier, new Hythe Quay and improved Town Quay landing steps provided during the early 1880's changed all this.

The New Forest too, gained a new entrance with Hythe Pier being sold as a "point of departure for the forest" by the contemporary press. The route received royal approval on August 13, 1888 when Prince and Princess Henry of Battenburg accompanied by Princess Alice of Hesse stepped onto the pierhead from their yacht, **Elfin,** bound for a long circular tour.

The Royal visit of 1888 paved the way for a flood of passengers en route for various parts of the New Forest. Visits like those of the members of the Winchester Town Council to Beaulieu on July 23, 1891 and on September 26 later the same year the Blue Cross Brigade's cycle run to Eaglehurst.

The ferry-boat **Hotspur** was gaily decorated and flew, on her bow, a flag bearing the Winchester coat of arms to mark the occasion of the crossing by the members of the Winchester Town Council and for the Blue Cross Brigade cyclist a special fare of one shilling return for man and bicycle was agreed by Mr. James Percy, by then, owner of the ferry-boats and lessee of the pier tolls.

The Hythe of the 1880's offered quaint narrow streets with aging cottages and interesting low ceilinged shops surrounded by field after field, with quiet woody lanes meandering betwixt. The company assisted in making Hythe worthy of a visit by making a six acre field near the tollhouse available for excursionists and ferry passengers alike to use for recreational purposes during the summer months of July, August and September, 1885, a practice repeated for several years thereafter.

It is hard to appreciate that Hythe and the New Forest could be so alien to the townsfolk of Southampton when we sit in our speedy motor cars eating up the miles along the wide dual carriageways that have been carved into some of this nation's most beautiful scenery and so difficult to feel the sense of adventure felt by those who did day trips into the area, now that places the like of Amsterdam, Brussels and Paris fall into the day trip category.

As well as seeing the good times the pier has witnessed moments of tragedy. Only 18 months after the official opening, on the morning of Sunday May 21, 1882 Hythe wherryman Edward Wall discovered a body hanging from an iron girder of the structure. The body was that of one John Gregson, a rivetter of Bishop Wearmouth, Sunderland, who had been involved in a fight the previous evening.

Oscar Ottell, a commercial traveller was the victim of an amazing accident during the evening of March 18, 1892. The steamer was just about to pull away from the pier when the captain noticed Ottell making his way along the structure to catch the boat. On arrival at the top of the steps he fell the full distance onto the platform below but managed to haul himself back onto his feet, albeit in a somewhat unsteady condition, only to fall again, this time over the edge and into the water. No time was wasted in fishing him out when it was found that he was unconscious.

The steamer Captain's awareness of the situation without doubt prolonged Oscar Ottell's life. Such reflexes were also possessed by Miss Evans, the daughter of Dr. Evans of Hythe. It was a fine Tuesday afternoon when on June 4, 1895 a pleasure boat being crewed by two women and a man capsized close by the pier. It was immediately evident that all three were in serious trouble as the fully clothed Miss Evans dived into the water. A large number of eye-witnesses watched as the gallant lady who being a splendid swimmer managed to save each of the three endangered souls.

The Pier has changed little in appearance over the years. Following its construction nothing other than replanking and strengthening was effected by design during it's 'youth' although the decision to

Early picture of Hythe Pier train mid 1920's.

allow the Hythe Sailing Club to use the Pier for it's premises brought about the provision of a clubhouse on the pierhead early in 1894. This innovation brought to the structure many elegant yachts and their equally distinguished owners, including Mrs. Gould's fine steam yacht **Atlanta** on September 5 later that year.

A massive £1,500 overhaul was completed towards the end of 1896. The work which included replanking from end to end was carried out by Messrs. Roe and Grace of Southampton.

Railway lines were layed down in 1909 for the purpose of running a hand propelled trolley to convey passengers' luggage and cargo from the ferry to the landward end of the structure. Further sidings were developed in the ensuing years.

An electric railway was introduced in 1922 and has operated to this present day.

The train was a godsend to the commuter traffic across the passage, although it was far from being a new idea. The plans lodged in 1870 had allowed for a railway to operate along the centre of the deck with a footway on the south side as well as that on the north as is the case today.

Other developments on the structure had taken place two years prior to the introduction of the railway, the most important being the construction of the Ticket Office to replace the old tollhouse which has been built with the pier in 1880 and still stands at the pier entrance. The pier entrance itself was considerably modernised during the early 1960's. Also during the sixties two shelters along the length of the pier were removed. Major developments were executed in 1947 to reconstruct the pierhead, including the pontoon being moved away from the pierhead, where it had been constructed during the early thirties, and connected by bridge. The pierhead buildings were extensively modernised and re-decorated during 1970-71.

All other work carried out on the structure has arisen from necessity. Major repair work was needed after being struck by the schooner rigged collier **Annie** which on July 30, 1885 came into contact with the pier midway along the north side as she was making a course towards her berth at Hythe Quay moving parallel to the structure. An investigation revealed that with the wind being fairly strong a slight miscalculation in the lowering of the sails brought about the collision. Five of the pier's cylindrical piles were either broken or carried away altogether. The piles came in for some further rough treatment during the severe winter of 1894—95. The unaccustomed sight of icefloes, some of more than two acres in extent, racing down Southampton Water and crashing into the piles gave considerable cause for concern. However, the winter passed and the following summer's repair programme was concentrated on the decking and joists. Not so lucky though was the 80 ton schooner **Jane Davies** which was at anchor just off Hythe Pier during the middle of February. A fast moving floe ripped her open and complete with her cargo of seed oil she sank immediately, the crew escaping but losing their effects.

About this period of time the facilities at the pier came in for criticism from a number of sources, the majority from wherrymen fighting a losing battle with the steamers. However, a more important criticism was made by a Trinity House pilot, who had written to the Southampton

July 8, 1952. Hythe Pier is put under strain as the crowds gather to witness the maiden arrival of the United States. (Southern Newspapers Ltd.)

Harbour Board informing them of his surprise that whilst in charge of the North German Lloyd liner **Neckar** on the night of May 10, 1885, he found that the lights of Hythe Pier were not lit.

Other collisions occurred in 1915 when the sailing barge **Itchen** came into contact with the structure causing it no damage while losing her own topmast and in 1945 when an LCP (Landing Craft, Personnel) damaged a number of piles.

The beginning of the twentieth century saw a number of Royal visits including those of King Alphonso XIII of Spain on April 27, 1906, Kaiser Wilhelm II of Germany on December 6, 1907, Princess Beatrice of Battenburg on August 25, 1909 and Prince and Princess Henry of Prussia on July 9, 1911. Another Royal visit, that of King George VI, took place just prior to D.Day in 1944. His Royal Highness rode the pier in the train.

Other great occasions of the present century include the **"Cleopatra"** entrances into Southampton of the Atlantic liners **Queen Mary** and **United States**. The arrival of the former on April 3, 1936 saw more than expected onto the pier as Hythe was flooded by an exceptionally high tide, but even those numbers couldn't compare with the arrival of the first post war leviathan, the United States. Never before, and likely never again, had such a sight as that of July 8, 1952 been seen in Southampton Water. Some estimates claim some 50,000 people to have witnessed the arrival, from the water, Weston Shore, Southampton Docks, the Hythe shoreline and from Hythe Pier. A contemporary photograph shows the piles of the structure almost bowing under the stress.

Although social activities have changed dramatically during the twentieth century, the pier still serves social needs beyond the ferry service. Almost every day of every summer draws the crowds to sample the excellent views of the big ships passing along Southampton Water that has been a feature since it's construction. There is a restaurant on the pierhead and despite the almost non-existence of good fishing, the ever patient anglers still line the structure. And there is still a spectacle in the Hythe calender with the pier very much involved.

The pier caters for many of the crowd which gathers to watch the annual challenge football match played by the Hythe firemen ON THE MUD to the south side of the pier behind the High Street. The match never fails to amuse the crowds both on the beach and the pier and provides the Fire Service's National Benevolent Fund with some much needed support.

100 years ago, Mr. J.H. Cooksey, Mayor of Southampton wished all those involved with Hythe Pier, a happy New year. Today, it's Happy New Century.

Pierhead developement 1971. (Alan Titheridge)

Boarding the train August 1935.

APPENDIX

Builders
Messrs. Bergheim & Co., London

Construction
1879—1880 (Official opening January 1, 1881)

Statistics
Length, (approx) 2,100 feet
Width (of pier proper) 16 feet
Surface Area (including pierhead) — approx 36,000 square feet
Height above high water — 4 feet (subject to normal tides)

Design
"The pier is composed of a pair of longitudinal wrought iron open girders, resting upon groups of cast-iron screw piles, 40 feet apart, and well tied by diagonal and other braces, the girders themselves being held together with cross girders of nearly equal strength". The deck was originally "formed of best pine joists, having the planks forming the floor, running in the direction of it's length." It has been relayed on numerous occasions, usually with "best English oak".

Contract Price
£7,700

Owners
Hythe Pier Co. Ltd. (formerly Hythe Pier and Hythe and Southampton Ferry Company Limited, pre-1923) registered on December 15, 1874.

A Victorian Vicennium 1881 - 1901

Each era of the Hythe Ferry's history has been very full, but none more so than the 20 years under discussion here.

Having, in the shape of Hythe Pier, provided the public of Hythe that much needed facility of a dry landing place, the Hythe Pier and Hythe and Southampton Ferry Company were now looking for the same at Southampton's Town Quay. The Town Quay landing steps had been widely criticized for a number of years. The project was to receive the whole-hearted support of the Southampton Harbour Board, but for 3½ years it became for it a major embarrassment. Southampton Harbour Board meetings became stormy as a succession of private plans were presented and rejected both emphatically and narrowly. Progress was being made, but not being seen to be so and consequently a mood of frustration arose both amongst those connected with the operation of the ferry and those patronising it.

The frustration was echoed in the press on May 14 1881 when the following appeared in the Southampton Times under the heading, "The Hythe Traffic."

> "It is a matter of regret that while on the Hythe side of the water great and expensive improvements have been made and are still going on, nothing has yet been done by the Harbour Board to increase the accommodation on this side. It is of the utmost importance, in the interests of enlarged traffic, that improved facilities should be provided at some point on our Quay line for the steamers plying between Southampton and Hythe. The question has been before the Harbour Commissioners: but hitherto nothing has been done. We hope the Board will realise the necessity of at once taking the matter in hand, and of making such arrangements as will conduce to the development of a not unimportant branch of local traffic."

Pier approaches known as The Bridge circa 1890.

The matter which had caused the Harbour Board so much frustration and embarrassment in the eyes of the general public was finally settled in a very controversial meeting on January 17, 1882. It was recommended that the Sun steps be carried out 22 feet with protecting piles from the first landing below the level of the Quay, which would be lengthened accordingly, the work to be done by the Harbour Board's own labour. After much passionate debate in which the guillotine was implemented, the scheme was carried but using outside labour and accepting Mr. Fry's offer to pay 10% of the costs.

Almost before the work had even begun, the Harbour Board found themselves locked in combat on another matter with the very people that they were providing the facilities for. Going through Parliament was the Southampton Harbour Bill, 1881, which had among its many clauses one to levy a toll on all passengers and goods landed at the Town Quay from Hythe. The Hythe company naturally objected and lodged a petition on February 25. The petition claimed that such a toll would deter many of the passengers from the passage and in due course the market for Hythe, Southampton, would suffer accordingly.

The objections came before the Court of References at the House of Commons on March 20 when it was decided that the locus standi sought by the company and Mr. Fry should be disallowed altogether which meant that the petitioners were banned from appearing before the Committee of the House of Commons. Both the company and Mr. Fry applied for a re-hearing of their petition which was heard at the House of Commons on April 18. Their council, explained that the objection was only against the clauses which imposed a new tax on the Hythe traffic. He felt that this had not been made absolutely clear during the original hearing. The Harbour Board's council, could only agree that it was a new tax and on this concession, the petitioners were allowed their locus standi.

Meeting on the same afternoon the Harbour Board heard their meeting chairman, remark,

> "the Hythe Pier Company had managed by hook or by crook to get the case re-opened."

He went on to say that the company did not have a leg to stand on but despite his confidence in the outcome of the London meeting the battle was now hotting up.

A public meeting to discuss the opposition was called at the Drummond Arms on April 29. After a few introductory remarks from Mr. Candy, Mr. E.A. Drummond, explained in great detail the special clauses of the bill and their effect on the people of Hythe. These clauses were regarded as being most unfortunate for both the publics of Hythe and of Southampton by Lord Henry Scott. In his lengthy speech, this gentleman said that as the Hythe people had been accustomed to trading with Southampton since time immemorial, the tolls were most unjust and that if sanctioned it would just be a matter of time before all trade had to go to Lymington. He made a concerned reference to the local agricultural interests before expressing his belief in the support of Southampton traders. As Mr. Fry was paying a percentage of the development costs of the Town Quay, Lord Henry Scott felt they were perfectly justified in their opposition and moved the following resolution.

> "that this meeting views with much regret and apprehension the attempt of the Southampton Harbour Board to impose a tax on the goods and passenger traffic between Hythe and Southampton, and pledges itself to resist the imposition of such a toll by every lawful means within it's power."

It was unanimously carried.

The Bill came before Parliament on May 16 when the normal ranks in the House were swelled by a vast contingent from both Hythe and Southampton. The proceedings were far too involved to even try to summerise, but the verdict was for the opponents. Evidence was presented by Lord Henry Scott, Mr. Fry and others during a monumental afternoon for the people of Hythe.

The Southampton Harbour Board took the decision to heart with one member expressing his feelings on June 24, that since their success in the House of Commons those connected with the Hythe traffic thought they could do as they liked.

There was no accommodation at the Town Quay for protection against the elements and only the weather side of a railway truck, regetfully all too infrequently available, relieved the misery of the passenger traffic during adverse conditions. Usually the nearest public house with a view was resorted to but although good for the establishment's business it was hardly what the public wanted. The obvious answer was a shelter of one sort or another and thereby arose another embarrassment for the Southampton Harbour Board. First proposed as early as November 19, 1889, when the argument against it was one of cost against the £5 annual nominal sum received from the Hythe Pier and Hythe and Southampton Ferry Company for the privilege of landing cattle, sheep etc. as well as some 120,000 plus passengers, a shelter was passed around from committee to board to committee until it finally materialised, again subsidised by the ferry boat proprietors, during the summer of 1901.

There were numerous other references to the company's interests made during Harbour Board meetings but these were dealt with with considerably less difficulty.

Mr. Fry was involved in an Admiralty case, the Isle of Wight Company versus Fry, on Januray 11, 1881. The case, which was heard at the Southampton County Court, arose from a collision between the Isle of Wight steamer **Prince Leopold** and Mr. Fry's **Louisa** on September 8, 1880. The Isle of Wight Company had filed a claim to recover the sum of £50 for damages to their vessel while Mr. Fry had made a counter claim for £35.

The Court heard that the 113 ton **Prince Leopold** was approaching the pontoon at the Royal Pier when her master, Captain Beazley, noticed the Hythe steamer coming out, only having time to order the reversal of his engine and give the order 'Hard a starboard' before being run into on the starboard bow. It was stressed that the collision was due simply to the negligence of the person in command of the **Louisa**, which had nobody in the bow. It was suggested that the **Louisa** took a shorter route out in order to make up a 9 minutes late start. In reply, Richard Banks, skipper

Town Quay, Southampton about the turn of the century.

of the **Louisa**, stated that he had taken the only course available to him as he had been doing for a week or more previous, (from different steps, his usual steps on the opposite side of the Quay being blocked). He held to round 3 bouys each with a vessel moored to it and had started late due to a vessel coming around the Town Quay Extension. Edward Blanchard, master of the tug **Fanny**, confirmed that the master of the **Louisa** had done nothing unusual, adding that he thought the vessel was moving at about 2 miles per hour. Two witnesses offered evidence that the **Prince Leopold** had been coming in at a considerable speed and had knocked a splinter off one of the piles of the new Town Quay Extension.

Judge Leonard, and his nautical assessors, concluded that both captains had contributed to the accident and that both had done their utmost to avoid it, but were beaten by lack of time. The verdict was for the defendent but with each party paying its' own costs.

The first AGM of the Hythe Pier and Hythe and Southampton Ferry Company following a year of active operations was held on February 7, 1881. The meeting was of a very formal nature with the only real point of interest being the decision to lease the pier tolls to Mr. Fry for a net annual rental in order to guarantee a fair dividend.

A general meeting was called on September 24 to discuss various matters requiring only formal resolutions. These included the leasing of the tolls to Mr. Fry for a further period and to enlarge and improve the landing stage on the pierhead in order to give better facilities to the larger vessels which called. The further lease granted to Mr. Fry was to commence from January 1, 1882 and run for a period of 3 years at terms which the gathering thought to be "very advantageous to the company".

It should be noted that in 1875, when the company's prospectus was issued, the number was taken at 92,000, by 1881 it had risen to 124,533 and in 1882 129,818. In 1883 the figure of passengers had risen to 131,876, an increase of 7,343 since the opening of the pier.

Early in 1884 an announcement in the London Gazette revealed an interesting situation. It would appear that the Board of Trade had written annually to the 1871 Hythe and Southampton Pier and Steam Ferry Company asking why their annual return had not been submitted, the letters always being re-addressed to the Hythe Pier and Hythe and Southampton Ferry Company Limited who of course had to reply that they had already sent theirs in. After 5 years it was realised by the Board of Trade that they were dealing with 2 separate concerns and so would give notice in the London Gazette of the dissolution of the 1871 company. Despite protests by the 1874 company that such an announcement might be detrimental to their business, this action was taken with the final nail being driven into the 1871 company's coffin on January 15, 1884.

1885 and 1886 were comparatively quiet years for the company, unlike 1887 which was to see the first major change in company policy since the re-constitution a decade previous. The 1887 AGM was held on February 7 and chaired by Mr. Drummond supported by Lord Montagu (formerly Lord Henry Scott). After the usual formalities had been disposed of Mr. Candy read the following report,

> "In meeting the shareholders for the seventh time since the opening of the pier, the directors are pleased to present a more favourable report than hitherto. The past year has been a comparitively uneventful one for the company but there are a few matters which require comment and

explanation. The balance sheet shows an important advance, though, as foreshadowed by the directors in their report, there has been a somewhat heavy outlay for repairs: but no work has been done but what was essential for the safety of the structure and the interest of shareholders. Several fender piles have been placed in position, and these, with the warping bouys which have been fixed, will greatly reduce the risk of collision of vessels passing alongside the pier and discharging at the quay. In these and other ways the directors have endeavoured to increase the utility of the pier and encourage traffic at a minimum of risk. One of the directors, namely, R.H. Hobart Esq. retires from the Board by rotation at this meeting, but offers himself for re-election. With regard to the future precuniary arrangements of the company, the directors have anxiously considered the subject, and having consulted those in a position to advise in such matters, they recommend the issue at an early date of £5000 in debentures bearing interest at 5 per cent per annum for the purpose of

(1) paying off the existing debenture issue of £4000 bearing interest at 6 per cent,

(2) of discharging the temporary loan of the bankers, and

(3) of preserving a reserve fund for contingencies.

It was not found practicable to borrow this sum on advantageous terms by means of a private mortgage, and the directors hope that the new debenture issue will be readily subscribed by the shareholders, and also taken in subscription for existing debentures. The necessary authority to carry out this arrangement will be obtained at a subsequent meeting, the details not being quite ready at the present time. But the whole matter must be completed and the bankers paid off not later than the 1st July next. The action brought agaist the company by the contractor, M. Bergheim, and his assignee has hitherto made little progress and the directors see no reason to alter their determination to resist the claim if the plaintiffs proceed. For obvious reasons it is advisable not to refer to the matter in general detail in this report. The most important item upon which the directors have to report is the new lease of the pier tolls. A very strong opinion having been expressed at the last two or three general meetings that the tolls should be put up to competition, the directors decided to adopt this course in view of the approaching termination of Mr. Fry's lease. Before doing so, however, they thought it only right to Mr. Fry to give him the option of continuing for another year at the rent which he had been paying, namely £520. Mr. Fry, however, did not see his way to accept the offer, and tenders were accordingly advertised for, resulting in the highest tender (that of Mr. Percy) being accepted. The lease is for three years, at a rent of £665 per annum, the lessee bearing all expense of lighting, cleaning etc. Mr. Percy's testimonials are of the most satisfactory character, and he has had a long experience both as a lessee of tolls and of a steam ferry. The directors are confident that the shareholders will fully approve of the conclusion of this arrangement, and also approve of the qualified promise which the directors have made to renew the lease at the end of three years at the same rent, if the covenant and conditions are properly performed. The Board, however, cannot sever their connections with Mr. Fry, as lessee of the tolls without cordially acknowledging his past services to the company and his efforts to promote the prosperity of the undertaking. The increased revenue which is now being earned will, it is hoped, enable and thus greatly improve the value of the company's ordinary share capital. The only other matter that requires comment is the bill of the Southampton Harbour Board brought in this session. The company's interests appear to be sufficiently protected and the victoy won in 1882 will not be wasted but at the same time the directors propose to carefully watch progress of the bill through Parliament to see that no amendments are introduced which will be injurious to the Pier company's interests. In conclusion the directors though the opening of the railway to Hythe and other looked for developments are still delayed, are glad to express continued confidence in the stability and ultimate success of the company's whole interests have been entrusted to their keeping.
The balance sheet is as follows:— Receipts — To capital, namely, 918 shares at £10 per share (less £80 arrears) £9,100; to amount received on debentures, £4,000; to creditors, £971 15s 11d; to suspense account (Bergheim & Co.) £13 7s 0d; to profit and loss, £254 7s 3d; total £13,340 0s 2d. Expenditure — By Parliamentary expenses, cost of erection of pier and buildings, and purchase of rights of the Hythe Hard Company, £14,198 0s 2d; by debtors, £142; total £14,340 0s 2d. The sum of £2,492 12s 6d claimed not acknowledged as a debt (Bergheim & Co.) is put down as a contingent liability."

Mr. James Percy's inception was to be that of a continuous interest by the Percy family in the affairs of the Hythe Ferry right up until this present day. He really became established on March 2, 1887, when he acquired both the **Frederica** and the **Louisa** from Mr. Fry for the sum of £475.

At the end of February, 1888 Mr. Percy placed an order with Messrs. Willoughby Bros. of Plymouth for a new steamer scheduled for delivery by July of the same year. The new vessel, which it was hoped would increase the volume of traffic, had been designed by Hythe naval architect C.P. Clayton who was about to prepare plans for a pontoon to be located at the Pier's head. These 2 innovations show just how determined Mr. Percy was to make good the opportunities open to him. The new steamer, particularly, would be a boon to the ferry as the ageing **Louisa** and **Frederica** dating from 1858 and 1863 respectively were most uncomfortable and equally uneconomical. Add the cost of this steamer to the £145 Mr. Percy was paying above that Mr. Fry had been paying for the lease of the Pier tolls, then there might be a reason for Mr. Fry's abstention from continuing the operation of the service. Perhaps Mr. Fry could not afford a new vessel with the competition for the lease of the tolls. He must also have had memories of the old 1855 Hythe and Southampton Steam Ferry Company to which he served as auditor during their brief existence, during which not only one but 2 new steamers could not save them.

Appropriately christened with the name of **Hotspur**, the new vessel arrived during the middle of April 1889 with Mr. Percy wasting no time in putting her into service. By today's standards the **Hotspur** was a pretty primitive vessel but even she made the **Louisa**, which she was built to replace, look positively naive.

Hotspur off Hythe Pier.

Messrs. F. Fry, J. Percy, W. Winckworth and Lord Henry Scott had one thing in common; they were unquestionably the leading figures in the development of the Hythe passage during the nineteenth century. Monumental were their efforts but they were, however, surpassed by one other, E.A. Drummond.

This gentleman was responsible more than any other for the construction of Hythe Pier and once built, it's early success. He acted his role of chairman of the Hythe Pier and Hythe and Southampton Ferry Company to the full, during the early days offering to forfeit any dividend due to him so that others could receive a reward on their more humble investments and later on, taking out large amounts in shares so that re-construction and maintenance work could be carried out on the company's property. He rarely missed a meeting, no matter how unimportant. He had time for everything, and everybody.

Mr. Edgar Atheling Drummond died at the Hotel Danieli in Venice, a few days after falling ill, on Wednesday May 10, 1893. His body was interned in the family vault at Fawley Church on Saturday May 20, after a spectacularly moving funeral and procession involving a coffin bearing woodman's trolley pulled by two black horses, five mourning coaches, numerous private cabs and carriages and a vast army of pedestrian mourners.

Tokens of mourning were displayed everywhere, blinds lowered, curtains drawn, shops closed either completely or partially and flags at both Fawley and Hythe flying at half-mast. Many friends and relations had travelled from London, they began their return journey on a special steamer which left Hythe Pier at 4.15 p.m.

At the next AGM on February 5, 1894, Mr. Andrew Drummond, the eldest son of the deceased was elected to take his father's place on the Board.

"The enterprise of the owners of the Hythe Ferry is to be commended" wrote a Southampton Times columnist. The occasion of this pat on the back? The entry into service of Mr. Percy's second new steamer, the **Hampton**, on May 4, 1894.

The vessel, which had been built by Messrs. Day, Summers & Co. at Northam, made a trial trip on Southampton Water and the Hamble River the previous afternoon. Luncheon was served in the first class cabin with Mr. Percy presiding. His guests included among others Lord Montagu (in his capacity as Chairman of the Hythe Pier and Hythe and Southampton Ferry Company), Alderman W. Bone J.P. (the Mayor of Southampton and Chairman of the Southampton Harbour Board) and Messrs. F.H Candy and G. Day (representing the builders).

After toasting the Queen, Lord Montagu to cries of "hear hear" spoke of the success that Mr. Percy had had in replacing the old **Louisa** and **Frederica** so soon after assuming his responsibility as lessee of the pier tolls. He thanked Mr. Percy for his hospitality that afternoon on behalf of all the guests and proposed "success to the **Hampton** and good health to Mr. Percy". Mr. Percy responded, saying that he trusted that the **Hampton** would become "a favourite with the public".

A most regrettable incident at the Town Quay occured on the dark stormy Saturday night of December 6, 1884.
As the steamer arrived at the Town Quay, David Batchelor proceeded as he had been doing for more than 20 years, to assist with her mooring but on reaching forward for the rope thrown to him from the vessel, he overbalanced into the water. The fast ebbing tide immediately carried the 61 years old man away from the quay with the terrible conditions making any rescue attempt quite impossible. Indeed, after hitting the water he was never actually sighted again. On the following Tuesday a reward was offered for the recovery of the body following the failings of an official recovery team. As far as has been possible to trace the reward was never claimed. David Batchelor had been a very popular man with both occasional and regular travellers alike.

The Southampton Harbour Board discussed the incident when they met on December 16, deciding after a debate on why there was not a grapling hook at the bottom of the quay to provide one.

There was plenty of incidents, in which the weather was to play a major role. A real "pea-souper" descended upon Southampton Water on November 11, 1888 throwing the activity of the port into total disarray. All ferry services both in and out were suspended but by 4 o'clock in the afternoon it was felt by the captain of the steam launch operating the reduced Sunday service that the fog was thinning and visibility was sufficient to take his vessel across from Hythe Pier to the Town Quay. With a large number of passengers aboard the launch left exactly on the hour. However, the fog increased in density and the journey took a little longer than the

Guests for trial trip of Hampton May 1894 including standing second left Mr F. H. Candy with son and seated left to right Mr J. Laurie (director), Lord (Henry Scott) Montagu, Mr James Percy and Alderman W. Bone (Mayor of Southampton).

usual 15 minutes. To be exact 2¾ hours longer. Shortly before 7 o'clock the many tired and frightened passengers were disembarked at Southampton after the slowest passage by steamer on record. Regular passengers had to endure several uncomfortable crossings during the Winter of 1888—1889; a very strong south-easterly made the water very choppy, sufficient to warrant the hoisting of the red danger flag on the Town Quay on December 21 and on January 5 another dense fog extended the passage time for the steamers to about an hour.

A "furious gale" on December 12, 1893 turned "the choppy wavelets which usually prevail when the water is rough" into "genuine rollers, such as might be expected on the shores of an open sea." The captain of the **Hotspur**, unable to return to Hythe against the almost violent gusts, decided that the Town Quay was not as protective as he would like so at 2.00 p.m. he took his command out into the comparitive safety of the Docks. This task which took more than 90 minutes to effect proved a wise move as several boats were lifted out of the water at the Town Quay, suffering severe damage. A similar gale blew on January 2, 1899 when after her last passage from Southampton the **Hampton** was unable to reach her moorings off Hythe Pier and had to spend the night in a very exposed position against the structure.

On January 7, 1893 the Sunday service met with a different weather problem. The steam launch could not operate until late in the day as her pipes and boiler froze up completely in the severe conditions.

There was plenty of incidents on nice days too. On a fine summer's day during the middle of July 1882, passengers awaiting the departure of the 11.30 a.m. boat from Hythe Pier were suddenly awaken from

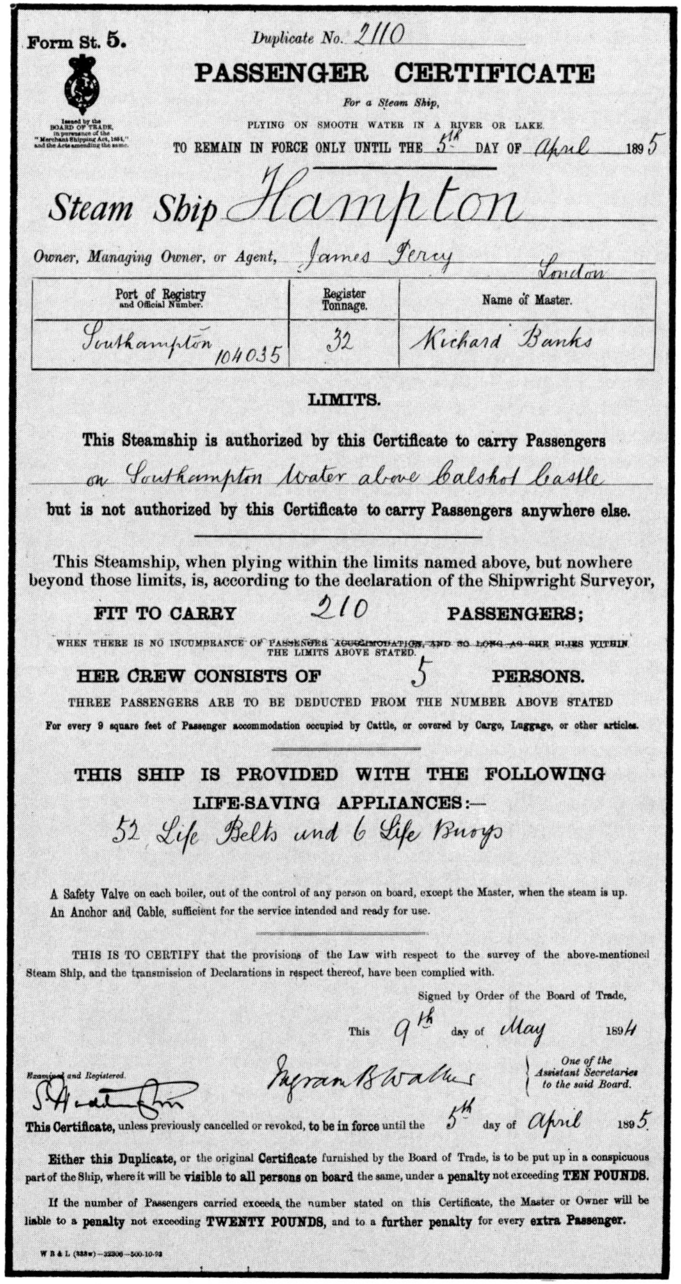

Form St. 5. Duplicate No. 2110

Issued by the BOARD OF TRADE, in pursuance of the "Merchant Shipping Act, 1854," and the Acts amending the same.

PASSENGER CERTIFICATE

For a Steam Ship,

PLYING ON SMOOTH WATER IN A RIVER OR LAKE.

TO REMAIN IN FORCE ONLY UNTIL THE 5th DAY OF April 1895

Steam Ship Hampton

Owner, Managing Owner, or Agent, James Percy London

Port of Registry and Official Number.	Register Tonnage.	Name of Master.
Southampton 104035	32	Richard Banks

LIMITS.

This Steamship is authorized by this Certificate to carry Passengers on Southampton Water above Calshot Castle but is not authorized by this Certificate to carry Passengers anywhere else.

This Steamship, when plying within the limits named above, but nowhere beyond those limits, is, according to the declaration of the Shipwright Surveyor,

FIT TO CARRY 210 PASSENGERS;

WHEN THERE IS NO INCUMBRANCE OF PASSENGER ~~ACCOMMODATION, AND SO LONG AS SHE PLIES WITHIN~~ THE LIMITS ABOVE STATED.

HER CREW CONSISTS OF 5 PERSONS.

THREE PASSENGERS ARE TO BE DEDUCTED FROM THE NUMBER ABOVE STATED For every 9 square feet of Passenger accommodation occupied by Cattle, or covered by Cargo, Luggage, or other articles.

THIS SHIP IS PROVIDED WITH THE FOLLOWING LIFE-SAVING APPLIANCES:—

52 Life Belts and 6 Life Buoys

A Safety Valve on each boiler, out of the control of any person on board, except the Master, when the steam is up.
An Anchor and Cable, sufficient for the service intended and ready for use.

THIS IS TO CERTIFY that the provisions of the Law with respect to the survey of the above-mentioned Steam Ship, and the transmission of Declarations in respect thereof, have been complied with.

Signed by Order of the Board of Trade,

This 9th day of May 1894

Examined and Registered. Ingram B Walker *One of the Assistant Secretaries to the said Board.*

This Certificate, unless previously cancelled or revoked, to be in force until the 5th day of April 1895.

Either this Duplicate, or the original Certificate furnished by the Board of Trade, is to be put up in a conspicuous part of the Ship, where it will be visible to all persons on board the same, under a penalty not exceeding TEN POUNDS.

If the number of Passengers carried exceeds the number stated on this Certificate, the Master or Owner will be liable to a penalty not exceeding TWENTY POUNDS, and to a further penalty for every extra Passenger.

W B & L (333w)—32300—500-10-93

Passenger Certificate Hampton May 1894.

their daily routine by a "madman" who according to a comtemporary report was "rushing about the boat and talking in the most random manner, and flourishing a knife, which he took from his pocket". Many passengers refused the crossing unless the crew ejected the man but the demands fell on stony ground as the crew decided it was not in their power to do so. Meanwhile a policeman who had been sent for as the situation grew out of hand arrived in his "civvies", overpowered the man, an ex-asylum inmate, and removed him from the ferry.

The limited Sunday service ran into an unexpected difficulty on October 16, 1887 which was to add armoury to those already involved in opposing the Sunday procedure of locking the Town Quay gates. Because of an extraordinary low tide the 2 o'clock steamer from Hythe had to land her passengers further along the quay due to the inaccessibility of her normal steps beyond the Town Quay gates. The disembarked passengers were most indignant to find themselves trapped on the Quay because of the locked gates and when it was realised that there was not an attendant let alone a key nearby, they voiced their opinions for all to hear. A crewman from the boat was dispatched in search of a solution but it was a considerable time before he returned with a key to release them from their temporary imprisonment.

During the afternoon of February 1, 1888 the Hythe steamer took on some extra custom at the Town Quay and immediately left for Hythe Pier, assuming the unlikely role of a fire engine. In answering a call to an outbreak at the home of a Mr. West in Hythe, the Southampton Borough Brigade sent a portion of it's crew across on the ferry while the appliance hurriedly left to make the long road journey via Totton, Marchwood and Dibden. The forwarding of the ferry party was an outstanding success as it had the fire out in time to stop the appliance at Totton.

Hampton on arrival at Southampton May 1894.

Poor lighting on the Town Quay landing steps was emphasized for the second time in the matter of only a few weeks when on January 23, 1889 an unfortunate gentleman, on leaving the last boat (6.00 p.m.) from Hythe, missed his footing and fell headlong into the water. As was in the earlier incident when a lady started this fad, there was an abundence of willing rescuers who speedily hauled him from his uncomfortable situation. After bringing himself to order the man was able to walk away, much to the relief of his rescuers and fellow passengers.

As the steamer was manoeuvering in close towards the Town Quay during the morning of September 20, 1889, eager to earn a few pence a street-boy leapt aboard before she was properly secured. The bare footed boy with a box on his shoulders missed his footing as he tried to step across to the quay from the rail of the boat which he had reached via a seat. He hit his head as he fell into the water and was apparently stunned. A gentleman who had witnessed the incident from the quay quickly realised the danger and leapt to the landing stage, laid down and by using his walking stick was able to reach the boy. The man managed to hold onto his catch until the boating hook called for, arrived.

Many people were driven from using the ferry during 1890 because of picketing. The Southampton labour strike which began on September 8 brought the Town Quay to a complete standstill, so in order to prevent any unofficial use of the strike-bound facilities anything that appeared vaguely suspicious, and not so suspicious, was intercepted and closely scrutinised. Although the Hythe traffic was something quite separate from the strike, the Town Quay steps being tendered by the company's own staff, many of the passengers had to suffer some of the inconvenience being forced upon the Town Quay's regular business. The searching of these persons and their property often resulting in the missing of a departure which of course led to frayed tempers, a few skirmishes and many complaints.

The ferry had matured considerably since the construction of the pier, but all so unnecessarily according to an opinion expressed by King Chulakongkorn I of Siam at a luncheon held in his honour at the Royal Pier pavillion on October 1, 1897, the twenty-ninth anniversary of his succession to the throne. "Having a very keen eye to business" his Majesty thought there ought to be a bridge across to Hythe. King Chulakongkorn was in town to inspect the renovation work being carried out on his 2,229 tons yacht, **M. Chakrkri**, by Messrs. Day. Summers & Co.

Another distinguished gentleman with ideas for the passage was the anonymous Southampton Town Councillor who wrote of a vision of 1920, 27 years on, in the Southampton Times for July 22, 1893. He wrote,

> "The Town Quay is much as of old, except that it's traffic has considerably increased. See, here is the cheapest penny trip in England. All the way to Hythe for one penny. Twenty-seven years ago the fare was fourpence, and that was not extortionate. The cheap fares originated in this way — a company of builders observing the congested state of Southampton, built about 500 cottages and villas at Hythe, and in order to fill those houses with suitable tennants they started the penny steamers. It was at first thought that the venture would prove a failure, but, as everyone knows, it is an immense success"

Through all the problems and successes of the era there was an atmosphere of warmth and expectation when life was generally uncomplicated. Although contributing nothing to the story of the Hythe Ferry it is perhaps typified by the scenes on and off Hythe Pier on August 27 and 28, 1895. the Hythe Sailing Club wound up it's racing season with a regatta on Tuesday 27. "There was quite a brilliant scene at the end of Hythe Pier, where the headquarters of the club are situated". Several exciting races were held and the gaily decorated clubhouse and Pier with the thronging audience enjoying the brilliant weather was quite a spectacle.

The mood continued over into the following day when again in splendid weather all Hythe was en fete for the annual Hythe Regatta. Moored alongside the Pier was the committee vessel, from which the races were started. Throughout the afternoon, an assortment of music was presented by the Beaulieu Brass Band.

There were races for various classes of boats including fishing boats (in which Mr. E. Baker "sailed over" to win in **Mayflower** in the under 25 feet class and Mr. H. Darwell won the under 18 feet class in **Vixen**). Mr. E. Pusey in **Doormat** won both the Yacht's Dinghy and Single Handed Fisherman races while Mr. J. Pickett jnr. in **Surprise** took the chequered flag in the under 14 feet Open Boat event. There were swimming events also; H. Stevens winning the boys race over 80 yards and W. Lawrence the mens over 100 yards.

Hampton arriving at Town Quay

The final event was a duck hunt with Mr. C. Bradford being "duck". To the pleasure of an appreciative crowd the "duck", several times climbed the piles, raced across the decking and dived back into the water to avoid being caught right until the whistle; his full 20 minutes "on the run" deserved the applause offered by the audience.

During the evening there was dancing following a concert presented by the band, both being well attended to conclude a very successful day.

1881—1901 were very successful years, very probably the 20 most successful years in the history of the Hythe-Southampton passage.

When Ted Low in his wherry, the **Blue Jacket**, gave up his David against Goliath act with the steamers, it was the end of an epoch. Before the introduction of steamers on the passage "you might take your choice of at least a dozen wherries" but the growing demand for both safety and speed pulled the loose around the wherryman's neck tighter and tighter, until with Ted Low it almost choked him. Finally, David succumbed to Goliath. This chapter tells something of the wherryman during his heyday, the period between 1820 and 1900. Licences were issued by the Southampton Harbour Board until recent years but this tells of the days when for/one would usually get/ and very often need,

Unknown boatman off Hythe Pier 1897.

Two bob, wet feet and an hour to spare.

The Hythe wherrymen were many in number during the 1820's but even so, with competition from the steamers a thing of the future, business was plentiful. There was, however, fierce competition among themselves for the additional revenue available for rowing passengers to and from the Isle of Wight steamers not able to gain direct access to the Town Quay. A number of warnings were issued by the Southampton Harbour Commissioners about the wherryman's over eagerness to get alongside, a dangerous, reckless practise in which many came to grief. To say that there was no love lost between the Isle of Wight steamer proprietors and the wherrymen would be an understatement. The steamers not only had the wherrymen swarming around for custom before berthing, but the latter continued to ply the waters in as carefree a manner as they had before the intrusion of steam communications. Incidents were to be commonplace as the master of the first Isle of Wighter, the **Prince Coburg**, was to find out very shortly after his vessel's commissioning. A Mr. Wiltshire of Frome and several woman passengers were tossed into the water as the wherry in which they were sailing capsized while cutting across the bow of the steamer. Engines were stopped immediately so that Mr. Wiltshire, his fellow passengers and the wherryman could be hauled from the water.

One of the first tasks undertaken by the Harbour Commissioners following their constitution in 1803, was to regulate the prodigious number of pleasure and ferry boats operating within their jurisdiction, including the Hythe wherries. With the growing number of steamers and increase of water transport following the abolition of landing dues in the early 1820's, such action was never more necessary. However, a motion was passed by the governing body in 1842 denouncing their authority over the Hythe—Southampton passage, but this was swiftly rectified by an Act of Parliament which had among it's clauses one calling for compulsory licencing of the wherryman to be re-introduced, 2 years later.

Our early nineteenth century heroes, in 1834, were obliged to display a plate, bearing their licence number, provided by the Commissioners on the backboard of their craft. Failure to do so meant a fine of 10s. (minimum) — £2 (maximum) for a first offence; £2 — £5 for a second; or £5 and a permanent suspension for a third. The wherryman also had to show the number of passengers that he was licenced to carry, which in no case would be more than 10. The fares for one passenger was 1 shilling, for two — 6d. each, for three — 4d. each and for four — 3d. each. No persons were to be detained while the wherryman waited for further passengers if those already aboard were prepared to pay the full fare. This latter ruling was, however, very often abused. If the weather was too boisterous, double the fare could be charged but only the Harbour Master had the authority to decide; his word being declared in the hoisting of a red flag on the Town Quay.

In 1852, the Hythe wherrymen were issued with armbands in the shape of a strap complete with a brass disc sporting either the Southampton Town Arms or the letters "SH" and the wherryman's official licence number. The practise of wearing these armbands was discontinued during the early 1900's and some of them have survived to this present day. Several wherrymen were reprimanded over the years for ignoring repeated reminders of the ruling despite it being a safeguard against the unsavoury reputation of some of the "pirate" boatmen who offered, in modern terminology, cut price excursions in what could only be described as questionable craft.

Until 1830, the wherryman had absolutely no opposition on the Hythe passage, but on March 10 of that year there came the first Hythe steamer, the **Emerald**. She was not a success, nor indeed were the **Forester** (1836—1840) or the **Gipsy** (1845—1847), so the wherrymen lost little. Their confidence, already high as the steamers failed was given a boost when the Directors of the Thames Iron Steam Boat Co. who arrived in Southampton by rail on May 11, 1840 to judge the viability of operating on the Hythe passage, left the same day without another word. In July 1855, the Hythe and Southampton Steam Ferry company was formed. Six years and 3 steamers later the company collapsed. But out of the ashes there rose a phoenix. This phoenix in the shape of William Winckworth, the former secretary of the now defunct concern, was to unconsciously start the wherryman's downfall. Mr. Winckworth's success was followed by that of Mr. Frederick Fry and Mr. James Percy. Hythe Pier, built in 1879—1880, while providing for the wherrymen was obviously designed to cater for the masses, and the masses preferred the comfort and now proven reliability of the steamers.

To add to their problems the Southampton Harbour Board over the latter years of the nineteenth century refused several licences until costly improvements to boats were effected, very often too costly for the wherryman to carry on.

It was during the 1850's that there came in the shape of the Hythe and Southampton Steam Ferry Company's steamers, the first real threat to the wherryman's livelihood. For reasons which do not appear to be on record the first of its steamers, the **Prince Alfred**, unlike the **Forester** and **Gipsy** which had operated to the Royal Pier, was placed on a station between Hythe and the Town Quay, at first much to the chagrin of the wherrymen. It was then realised that the **Prince Alfred** would often have to call upon the wherrymen to carry her passengers to and from the shore. It might appear sense to have used a wherry for the whole passage, but as the following will show the inconvenience at the Town Quay was minimal. In promoting the Hythe and Southampton Steam Ferry Company a contemporary reporter wrote, "we were rowed across recently against the tide and with no wind, and took one hour."

Despite the failings of the Hythe and Southampton Steam Ferry Company, there was never again to be a time without steam communication. William Winckworth's success with his two steamer service was really the writing on the wall for the wherrymen, whose estimated total of 60,000 passengers in 1847 dropped to only 9,000 in 1865. The wherrymen were, however, still very much involved with the Hythe passage.

On Saturday February 1, 1873, two keepers from the Royal mail Company's steamship **Oneida** lying up off Netley had gone ashore to Southampton to fetch provisions. The two men packed their small sailing craft and at 5 o'clock in the afternoon left the Town Quay to return to the **Oneida**. They never reached their destination, their craft being discovered with sail down and mast up by Dibden labourer Thomas King a half mile above the Hythe Hard the following morning. The two men were found sitting upright on their seats with their mouths and eyes wide open. Hythe wherryman John Banks, a member of the jury that deliberated the men to have suffered "death from exposure" during an inquest on February 3, spoke of the conditions on the fateful night. It would appear that the prevailing fresh breeze blew up into a blinding blizzard with the fast ebbing tide carrying the men to their deaths. Another Hythe wherryman, Henry Diaper, told of how it had taken him over 2 hours to free himself after having gone aground during the worst of the night. This last mentioned incident is surely a testimonial to the skill and determination of the regular Hythe wherryman.

During the Southampton Harbour and Pier Board meeting held on April 15, 1873 one of the wherryman was refused a licence following complaints about his continual overcharging and overcrowding. It was at this time that severe pressure was brought upon the wherrymen to improve the standard of their boats and equipment. The Harbour and Pier Board began to withhold licences to enforce this.

However, the wherrymen often allowed themselves as on September 12, 1873, a day to forget their worries and stage their own Waterman's Regatta. For the record, the result of the Sailing Wherry Race was:— 1st. **Johnny Broom** (R. Carey), 2nd. **Volante** (I. Blandford). 3rd. **Sphinx** (R. Edwards), 4th. **Dibden** (H. Blandford), 5th **Luck All** (J. Short), 6th. **Young Ocean** (G. Skanes) and 7th **Jane** (T. Blandford).

Some of the wherrymen were great characters. One, Edward Wall managed to hit the headlines no less than five times during the 1880's. The first was on the morning of Sunday May 21, 1882 when at about 8.20 while setting out for his day's work he found a body hanging from one of the Hythe Pier's iron girders.

If anybody was accident prone it was Edward Wall. On February 27, 1883 he slipped and fell in the street and sustained a fracture of the leg. He did an encore during the night of May 20/21, 1887 when after laying in Castle Lane, Southampton for a considerable time unable to get up and walk he was found by the Police at 4 o'clock. It was found that a small bone in his leg was broken, but fortunately he wasn't to be detained in hospital for too long before being allowed to return to his home at Sherbourne Villa in the High Street at Hythe. If all this wasn't enough he endured during the evening of September 17 later in the year, an experience that he must have remembered for the rest of his life.

A gentleman named Johnson who was staying at the Kelways Hotel in Terminus Terrace, Southampton arrived on the Town Quay seeking transport to Hythe. He eventually engaged Edward Wall who chose to use his small punt for the crossing. The Sky was very black but the water remained quite calm. All went well until the tiny craft was about halfway across when the occupants saw the 8 o'clock steamer from Cowes, the **Her Majesty**, bearing down on them. The conditions prevented the steamer captain from seeing the punt until he was almost upon it. Sensing the danger of collision the captain stopped his engines while the two men in the punt leapt clear into the water. A boat was promptly dispatched from the **Her Majesty** and picked up Mr. Johnson while the wherryman was rescued by a boat sent from the Duke of Bedford's yacht, the **Northumbria**. Both men were taken to the Royal Pier aboard the **Her Majesty** from where they were sent for medical attention. Mr. Johnson was released immediately but for Edward Wall who as well as being quite delirious suffered heavy bruising of an arm, it meant a few more days in hospital.

Just exactly what affect this incident had upon him we will never know, nor whether it brought about the scenes on the night of Sunday 25 when following an incident at the Wheelwright's Arms public house at Hythe, he was charged with being drunk and disorderly and further with causing damage to a door and breaking a window.

With a young companion Edward Wall was brought before the Hythe Petty Sessions held at the Drummond Arms the following Thursday, October 1. After hearing evidence from both William Long, landlord of the Wheelwright's Arms, and another man, the Bench imposed fines totalling £2 8s 9d. (including costs) on each of the defendents with an alternative of six weeks hard labour. The prisoners' attitude to the court probably added to their punishment, for during the hearing both continually interrupted the proceedings and on one constable's demand for "silence" Edward Wall replied,

> "keep your place, anyone would think you were the boss of the court."

He even had the audacity to ask for time to pay his fine but on refusal settled up with the Clerk from his pocket.

Another of the wherrymen was George Harris. His vessel, the **Johnny Broom**, was severely damaged when the **Hotspur**, which hadn't been on the passage more than a few weeks, ran into a cluster of wherries soliciting business at the Town Quay during the afternoon of June 13, 1889. Several other boats, one in particular belonging to James Paskins, suffered considerable damage also. It is believed that the misinterpretation of an order took the ferry on and not astern.

Mr. Percy introduced the **Hampton** to the passage in 1894 and together the **Hampton** and the **Hotspur** went from strength to strength. The plight of the wherryman was painfully obvious even then. It is difficult in this day of highly automated labour saving machinery to appreciate exactly what the wherryman was putting into the passage. His efforts in the first instant encouraged the passage. Had he not persisted when the early steamers had given up then the passage would be nothing more than a note in a history book.

Therefore, the regular patrons of the modern ferry owe him much. He was more than something special, he was the Hythe Ferry.

NOTICE.

TO PASSENGERS, CARRIERS, AND OTHERS.

The Hythe Steamers will leave the Hythe Pier and Town Quay punctually at the advertised times.

Passengers with luggage should be ready to embark five minutes before the Steamer is timed to leave.

Carriers and others having large quantities of parcels and goods to embark, should be ready to load up as soon as the steamer arrives, as otherwise part of their goods must be left behind for the next trip.

As these regulations are framed for the convenience of passengers, the Proprietor hopes for the assistance of passengers in carrying them out.

Dated, 1902. **(Signed) JAMES PERCY, Proprietor.**

Notice to passengers, Carriers and Others, 1902.

When the century was young 1901 - 1914

The twentieth century started tragically for the Hythe Pier and Hythe and Southampton Ferry Company. Having lost the services of director Mr. Henry Pigeon through death on July 19, 1898, they were to be stunned by the deaths of 2 even more active servants during April 1901.

Mr. James Laurie, another director was drowned whilst sailing on the morning of April 4. Mr. Laurie who was keen on sailing and respected in the locality for his interest in yachting came to grief just outside Cadland Creek.

The deceased, a former bank worker, had been land steward to the Drummond Estate for a little under 26 years, was 54 years old and had been a director of the Hythe company since 1891 although his association with it's interests date back many years previous.

The second of the April tragedies befell Mr. F.H. Candy, the company's secretary and solicitor, who died peacefully on the twenty-third. Mr. Candy was born in Bombay, India in 1845. He began his working life as a clerk in a customs office and was subsequently articled to Oxford solicitors, with whom he served his apprenticeship in the legal profession. He came to Southampton in 1874 and entered into partnership with Mr. William Perkins. When the partnership was dissolved after only 6 years he continued alone but for only a short while until he entered another partnership, this time with his cousin, Mr. C.H.H. Candy until his death.

Mr. Candy became the secretary of the Hythe company shortly after it's constitution.

During 1901 the Town Quay landing steps had been brought to the notice of the Southampton Harbour Board. There had been a number of complaints from the travelling public and on investigation it was undertaken by the Harbour Board, to carry out modification work by tender. As was always when this vexed traffic was under discussion, affairs took their time and work was not completed until the late Summer of 1902.

A situation arose late in 1902 that although at the time did not involve the Hythe steamers, resulted in them having to fall in line with a new bye-law affecting every other steamer in the Docks area. At a meeting of the Southampton Harbour Board on October 21 complaints were read about the speed of excursion steamers within the harbour. It was subsequently resolved that "no vessel propelled by steam or mechanical power shall proceed at a greater speed than six knots per hour above or to the northward of an imaginary line drawn from Hythe Pier to the Weston Shelf Gas Bouy". So far as the Hythe steamers were concerned, there were to be no problems.

An inquiry was held at the Oddfellows Hall, Hythe on March 27, 1903 into the London and South Western Railway Company's application for an Order to build a light railway from Totton to Stone. The meeting lasted for 6½ hours. The Hon. A. Lyttleton opposed the application on behalf of the Hythe Pier and Hythe and Southampton Ferry Company, and the Drummond Estate.

In opening the debate, Mr. E. Page K.C. representing the promotors reminded the meeting that it was as long ago as 1882 that Parliament authorised a similar construction promoted by the Swindon, Marlborough and Andover Railway Company. The promotors could not, however, raise the necessary funds even with an extension to the time limit.

"Surely," exclaimed Mr. Page, "if such a line were considered necessary 20 years ago it was needed at the present time to give facilities to 6000 persons living in the district."

Mr. Lyttleton contested that the population had not increased since 1882 but Mr. Page replied that it would never increase so long as it was being served as it was at that time (1903).

"How," he asked, "could a district prosper when they took into consideration the Hythe ferry boats which did not serve the public as they ought to be served?"

Sir Robert Hobart and Mr. C.H.H. Candy (who had succeeded his cousin into the firm) spoke on behalf of the Hythe Company.

On the promotors concession to abandon the section beyond Fawley, the Drummond Estate withdrew their opposition, before the Order was approved.

During a meeting of the Southampton Harbour Board on June 16, 1903 a report regarding rents charged on Harbour Board property was discussed. One of it's recommendations was "considering the additional accommodation now provided at the Town Quay for the Hythe steamers and their cargo and the increase of such traffic, the annual amount payable by the

company be increased to £25 per annum." The members of the Harbour Board were reminded of the previous attempt to impose an increased rent on the Town Quay steps which the Hythe company successfully contested on the grounds of a right to a landing there. Since then, however, a sum of some £400 had been spent on developing the site and that alone justified a higher rent than the £5 per annum then being asked.
On November 17 the new rental was adopted.

Meanwhile, away from the politics, the everyday life on or by the water continued, but not without it's incident.

Pierhead scene Summer 1903.

The Summer of 1903 was weather wise one to remember. The sun brought the people out and the water was still as popular as ever. Whitsuntide "being exceptionally fine and warm" meant that "the **Hampton** and **Hotspur** were filled to their utmost capacity on many of the trips" and on August Bank Holiday Monday (3) "the steamboats plying between Southampton and Hythe were well filled for each crossing."

The incident referred to above involved one of the remaining wherrymen, William Pusey (who described himself as a seaman and only plyed the passage occasionally). At about a quarter to eight during the evening of Saturday May 9 he set up a table in the middle of the road directly in front of the Pier gates and started to perform sleight-of-hand tricks.
A crowd about 100 strong quickly assembled, causing a carriage difficulties in getting away from the tollhouse.
A policeman asked William Pusey to move on five occasions, the only response being a grimace. As he (William Pusey) lit his pipe he was told by the Constable that unless he moved he would be locked up. The policeman then beckoned the people to disperse but as he moved away they turned hostile, hissed and chanted "rats".

William Pusey was brought before the Hythe Petty Sessions held at the Police Station on May 28 to answer a charge of obstructing the highway. After hearing the evidence, not all of which was admitted by the defendent as being true, Lord Montagu, the magistrate, imposed a fine of 1s. with 4s. costs.

The ferry carried a number of parties during 1904 and 1905, all of which provided useful income for Mr. Percy who was already enjoying business better than ever before. In addition Mr. Percy even laid on "a very convenient special service for Whitsuntide" (1904).

NOTICE - ON BANK HOLIDAY
THE
HYTHE STEAMBOATS
Will leave
SOUTHAMPTON:-
9.0, 9.30, 10.0, 10.30, 11.0, 11.30 A.M.
12.15, 1.15, 1.45, 2.15, 2.45, 3.15,
3.45, 4.45, 5.15, 6.0, 6.30, 7.0, 7.30,
8.0, 8.30 P.M.
Will leave
HYTHE:-
8.0, 9.0, 9.30, 10.0, 10.30, 11.0,
11.30 A.M., 12.15, 1.15, 1.45, 2.15,
2.45, 3.15, 3.45, 4.15, 5.15, 6.0, 6.30,
7.0, 7.30, 8.0 P.M.

A party of over 100 adults and children left Hythe on the 1.15 p.m. steamer for the Hythe Congregational Church Sunday School annual outing on August 3, 1904. Tea was served at 4 o'clock after which games were played for prizes of sweets. The Southampton Police Band arrived at 7 o'clock and played until the party left for home at about a quarter to eight.
Voyaging on the 8.15 p.m. steamer was a rare treat for the casual traveller, for the children gave a fine rendition of several well known hymns and songs and finally shouted cheers for the teachers, captain and crew. Children were also carried in number on Ocotober 26 for the Congregational Church Young People and

Junior Society of Christian Endeavour C.E. Rally held at Hythe during the early evening.

Mr. Percy speedily laid on a special boat at 11.00 p.m. so that the large crowds that had gathered to attend the garden fete at the Villa Amalthea, Hythe on August 31 which had to be postponed at the last minute as the torrential rain showed no signs of easing off, could spend the evening in the theatres of Southampton. The event was held the following day, when in opening the fete, Sir Robert Hobart spoke of his life long association with Hythe and in particular Langdown,

> "How many here, I wonder, besides myself, can remember the days before there was a Hythe steamer, when some 20 boatmen or more stood along the village street and touted for custom to go to Southampton, and elsewhere".

An event staged at the Hythe Petty Sessions in November 1904 saw Mr. Charles Wild presented with the honourary testimonial of the Royal Humane Society by Lord Montagu. It would appear that Mr. Wild had dived off Hythe Pier and managed to save the life of a woman in danger of drowning. The rescue, said Lord Montagu, not only conferred honour upon Mr. Wild, but upon the whole district.

Mr. Henry Richard Hall who had for a number of years been operating a steam launch between the Town Quay and Hythe Pier in competition with the steamers, died after a long illness on May 14, 1905. Mr. Hall was a former Southampton wherryman who had owned the wherry **Nil Desperandum** in August 1882.

A severe blow was dealt to the Hythe Pier and Hythe and Southampton Ferry Company on November 4, 1905. Lord Montagu who when Lord Henry Scott had

View of Wilts and Dorset Bank and General Stores in the Marsh circa 1905.

re-constituted the company with Mr. E.A. Drummond in 1877 and had served continuously as a director thereafter, (including 12 years as chairman following the death of Mr. Drummond), died at Palace House through heart failure after having been taken ill on August 28 with a lung infection, an ailment that had plagued him since childhood.

Lord Henry was born on November 5, 1832 the second son of the fifth Duke of Buccleuch. He was educated at Eton but could not finish his studies through ill health, the same lung trouble that led to his death, and had to travel abroad to a warmer climate for seven consecutive winters until strong enough to withstand one British style. During his youth and early manhood he was a conscientious student of Egyptology and travelled up the Nile on no less than seven occasions.

He sat in the House of Commons for Selkirkshire from 1861 until 1868 when he stood for South Hants and secured what was already a very safe seat. He held the seat until the peerage of the Baronry of Montagu was created by Queen Victoria on November 29, 1885.

His marriage to Lady Stuart -Wortley took place on August 1, 1865 and produced four children, including John Walter Edward (his heir). The Beaulieu Estate was received as a wedding present from his father. Lord Henry took up residence in Palace House during 1867 and soon recognised both the commoner's rights and the beauty of the New Forest.

The death of the first Baron Montagu was mourned nationwide. Telegrams of sympathy were received at Palace House from HRH King Edward VII, the Hon. A.J. Balfour M.P. (Prime Minister), Archbishop Davidson of Canterbury and many others. The funeral was held at Beaulieu Abbey on November 8.

A concert held on January 3, 1906 at the Oddfellows Hall, Hythe in aid of the Mayor of Southampton's fund for relief to the widows and orphans of the 27 seamen who died in the sinking of the **Hilda** on passage between Southampton and St. Malo on November 18, 1905, attracted over 300 persons many of whom came over the water to be present. Mr. Sturgess, who had been appointed manager of the Hythe steamboats by Mr. Percy, transported the artists, across the ferry for both rehearsals and the performance free of charge. The concert, was an outstanding success and raised £8 5s 6d. which was officially handed over to the Mayor a few days later.

The friendly atmosphere present on the concert night turned a little hostile in the Oddfellows Hall on January 15 during a meeting held there in the interest of the prospective Liberal Party Candidate for the New Forest. Hythe had never before taken much interest in General Elections, but that of January 1906 was of special interest. The constituency was predominantly Conservative but this time around the Liberals really felt they had something more than just an outside chance. Couple that to the fact that the prospective Liberal Candidate was Sir Robert Hobart, a director of the Hythe Pier and Hythe and Southampton Ferry Company and one of the oldest residents of Hythe, and the feeling in this quiet corner of England can be appreciated. Nobody, however, could have envisaged the scenes about to take place.

After Sir Robert had delivered his address, the meeting was offered to the floor for debate. During the debate, the Conservative Party sub-agent, a local magistrate, challenged Sir Robert on the question of Ireland, as delicate a situation then as it is today. Sir Robert's reply was not that sought by the questioner who rushed onto the platform and siezed hold of the 69 years old Liberal candidate. Sir Robert's supporters immediately intervened to protect him but scenes ensued the like of which had never been witnessed in Hythe before. The assailant was eventually ejected from the Hall by his friends, quite forcibly by all accounts, before order was restored and the incident formally condemned.

Reprisals were attempted during a similar event held in the interest of Sir Robert's Conservative opponent, at the Oddfellows Hall, Totton later in the week but the rowdy Liberal supporters were unsuccessful in trying to break up that meeting.

Feeling in Hythe grew stronger and stronger as each day passed. The poll took place on January 22 with the result (below) being announced the following day.

Sir R.H. Hobart (Liberal)	4,949 votes
Mr. H.F. Compton (Conservative)	4,901 votes
Majority	48 votes

News of the result spread quickly through the village and almost equally as fast crowds assembled outside Sir Robert's Langdown home. As Sir Robert had not returned from the official declaration the crowd waited, all the while growing in number. A car was seen moving towards the house and cries of "here he comes" excited the crowd but the car contained only Mr. Frederick Fry, a life long Liberal and the leader of the Hythe and Fawley Liberal Group, who was given tremendous applause as he passed. Sir Robert's car arrived a few minutes later and stopped so that the new M.P. could acknowledge the cheers and shake the hands of some of his supporters. His car then moved on into

Corner of Shore Road and South Street, circa 1910.

Marsh Street looking north....

the village and stopped at the Pier gates, where another large crowd of jubilant Liberals had assembled.

During the evening a torch-light procession singing "we've won this time, with Robert at the top of the poll" to the tune of a contemporary "hit", descended upon Sir Robert's home. The singing and cheering quickly brought Sir Robert, to the door. Sir Robert then addressed the crowd which, after rendering a chorus of "For he's a jolly good fellow" turned and marched towards the village still singing and cheering until they arrived at Mr. Fry's home, where they called for him to appear, before they dispersed in an orderly manner.

Sir Robert served the New Forest constituency until defeated at the next General Election, polling for which took place on January 25, 1910. The steamers were "feeling the effect of the election and continually carrying to and fro votes from Southampton and district".

.... and south circa 1906.

Result,

Mr. W.F. Perkins (Conservative and Unionist)	6516 votes
Sir R.H. Hobart (Liberal)	4423 votes
Majority	2093 votes

Hythe quickly returned to normality after the poll of January 1906 with the next couple of months passing uneventfully. There was just one incident, on April 24, which commanded no more than a few lines in the contemporary press. A motor launch which had just pulled away from Hythe Quay collided at full speed with one of the Pier's piles after it's steering gear had broken down. The engines were speedily shut down and the craft inspected for damage; the breaking of the ensign staff and hood framework being the full extent, the occupants suffering nothing more than shock.

King Alphonso XIII's launch arriving at Hythe Pier April 27 1906.

On April 27, Hythe Pier was used by King Alfonso XIII of Spain and his party on route to Highcliffe Castle from their accommodation at Osbourne Castle and again during their return later in the day. Just before 11 o'clock an Admiralty launch arrived at the pierhead and word was dispatched to the waiting cars, hidden away in the grounds of the Drummond Arms Hotel. The Launch, so obviously out of place, attracted a curious crowd. A contemporary reporter describes the setting,

> "The scene from Hythe Pier at 11 o'clock was varied and pleasing indeed. The dull grey hulls of the troopships lying off Netley stood out boldly against the background of vivid green of the Hamble shore. Up and down the fairway moved vessels ranging in size from the big coastal steamers connecting Southampton with Ireland and Scotland, to the black fishing craft of the forest boatmen. An early season yachtsman occasionally brought his vessel with white wings spread and brasswork glistening brightly, alongside the Pier and in and among the assorted shipping of the estuary".

At about 12.50 p.m. a destroyer dropped anchor off the Pier and the Admiralty launch went alongside to fetch the Royal Party. Meanwhile, the cars were being removed from the Drummond Arms and arranged inside the Pier gates.

The curious crowd had now grown into an excited multitude, with over 100 schoolchildren among them. King Alfonso ambled along the quarter mile Pier to receive a thunderous ovation as he and his entourage climbed into the waiting vehicles.

The procession travelled to Highcliffe via Beaulieu and Lymington, a route which in all probability brought back memories for the Spanish King. On a previous tour with the then Hon. J. Scott-Montagu their car was halted, quite dictatorially, by the old keeper of the Lymington toll-bar. The toll was paid as the man complained that two motorists had already "rushed" the bar and that he wasn't going to be "had" a third time. He did not, of course, know the identity of the gentlemen in the car, (nor would he believe it when subsequently enlightened), and insisted upon the car waiting still further while a donkey cart passed. The occasion of April 27, 1906 presented no such problem.

King Alfonso returned to Madrid a few days later to prepare for his wedding on May 31, an event sadly marred by an unsuccessful assassination attempt.

More than a year was to pass before anything worthy of note again elapsed. One note in passing though; the Hythe Regatta held on September 19, 1906 staged the earliest recorded "Football on the Mud" match, the "Muddy Muddlers" versus the "Mud Slingers". On August 3, 1907, the South Midland Volunteer Infantry Brigade, some 2,500 men in number, arrived for their annual training camp at Beaulieu. Harry Banks, the captain of the Hythe steamer, really had his work cut out on August 4. Being a Sunday, many of the soldiers took advantage of the fine weather and some free time to go to Southampton. On one occasion there were as many as 500 parading Hythe Pier and the village streets. The following day, too, was very busy, "two steamers were employed instead of one and they were well filled with each journey".

During the latter part of November 1907 Hythe Pier was made available by Mr. Percy for use at no charge by the crew of the steam yacht **Hohenzollern**, at anchor off Netley, and the servants of it's owner, Kaiser Wilhelm II of Germany, who was staying at Highcliffe Castle. Inquiries were made by the Commander of the **Hohenzollern** as to the depth of the water at Hythe Pier and from this it was deduced by the contemporary press that the Kaiser would return to his yacht via the Pier. The Kaiser did employ the Pier on December 6 but not exactly as the press had anticipated.

He left Highcliffe Castle for Hythe at 10.45 a.m. Meanwhile, the (Marine Superintendant of Southampton Docks left Southampton for Hythe in a motor launch to join Lord Montagu and others at the Hythe Pier gates to complete a reception party at 11.15. By this time a considerable crowd had also assembled. The Kaiser's car arrived at 11.28 and immediately he alighted and shook hands with each of the reception party before strolling along the Pier to the sounds of the cheering crowd. A voice from the crowd called for "three cheers for the emporer", which was of course taken up and acknowledged by the Kaiser with the raising of his military peaked cap.

To the surprise of the crowd the Royal launch, (from the **Hohenzollern**), did not head south towards the royal yacht but moved north towards the Docks with the Marine Superintendant's motor launch containing Lord Montagu and the Kaiser's retinue following behind. After completing a tour of the Docks the Royal launch did head south and to the firing of a salute the Kaiser stepped aboard his yacht at 12.48.

Although nothing official had been announced, the large crowd remained on or in the vicinity of Hythe Pier and were joined during the mid-afternoon by Sir Robert Hobart. At 3.58 the ensign on the mainmast of the **Hohenzollern** was lowered to signify the departure of Kaiser Wilhelm. As the Kaiser approached Hythe Pier two things happened that could so easily have ruined what was obviously a well organised programme. The Hythe steamer complete with a large complement of passengers arrived but was ordered to lay off until the Kaiser was clear of the Pier and about 50 schoolchildren at the end of their day's schooling ran down Hythe Pier cheering and quite out of order, but again the officials speedily came up with a solution. A few minutes later, the Kaiser stepped onto the Pier landing stage which had been covered with rubber non-slip pads by German "Bluejackets". A slip gangway covered with carpet was also employed. The Kaiser then made his way, again to cheers from the crowd, back to his waiting car and onto Highcliffe Castle.

During February 1909 it was announced that tramlines were to be layed down along the length of Hythe Pier, "for the conveyance of luggage etc." Previously, solid wheel trucks were in use and it was because of the damage done to the planking by these trucks that the investment in the tramway was decided upon. Mr. E.J. Kingham, who included being a local undertaker and funeral adviser among his many talents, secured the contract. Work began during early March and was completed by the middle of June; the sunken lines were not however, brought into immediate use. The tramway was put into service about a month later with the Hampshire Independent for July 31 reporting that "luggage and goods etc. are conveyed up and down on a couple of up-to-date trolleys". It was such a success that Mr. Kingham's workmen were re-employed during February 1910 to lay additional sidings so that the tracks could offer even more facilities to an appreciative public.

Tracks laid on Pier by Mr Kingham's workmen in 1909

Among the many parties to use the facilities offered by both Mr. Percy and the Hythe Company during 1909 was a company of the Royal Marine Artillery who crossed from Southampton to Hythe during the afternoon of June 11 and on landing on the Pier marched along it's length and onto their Beaulieu camp. Princess Henry of Battenburg made another of her frequent visits to the locality, landing at Hythe Pier, on August 25 for the occasion of Colonel C.V.C. Hobart's garden party at his residence at West Cliff Hall. The Princess stayed a little over an hour before returning to Cowes aboard her yacht, **Sheila.**

The weather considerably hampered the operation of the steamers during the Winter of 1910/1911. High winds prevailed for the best part of a week finally easing off on December 17, only to be followed by foggy nights that often carried over the following mornings. The fog on December 22 inconvenienced the traffic severely. Several of the early departures made the passage to schedule but the 10.30 a.m. from Hythe did not arrive at the Town Quay until after 11 o'clock. Harry Banks who had had to call upon his vast experience to make that passage did not venture out again until the fog lifted, during the mid-afternoon.

High Street looking towards Drummond Arms July 1907.

Hythe was full of excitement on Sunday July 9, 1911. That morning the members of the British and German teams representing the Royal Automobile Club and the Imperial Automobile Club who had enjoyed a successful 3 days competition in Northern Germany for a trophy presented by Prince Henry of Prussia, arrived at Southampton in magnificent weather aboard the North German Lloyd liner **Grosser Kurfust** which had been chartered to convey the motor cars from Bremerhaven. At the invitation of Lord Montagu, Prince and Princess Henry, the Duke and Duchess of Santona and the competitors, numbering over 500 persons in total, visited Beaulieu, the Abbey and Palace House on the morning of their arrival. Cars were specially requisitioned for the day by the Hants Automobile Club and placed inside the Hythe Pier gates to wait for their passengers, whose route to Beaulieu was via Hythe and it's Pier.
At one time during the morning there were as many as 80 cars there. Sir Thomas Lipton's steam launch was made available to bring over Prince and Princess Henry and Colonel C.V.C. Hobart's steam launch, **Ysolt**, and the Hythe steamers to bring the other guests. The latter made the return arrangements; depositing their passengers at the Ocean Quay in Southampton Docks during the early evening. The whole of the operation from conception to completion was faultlessly arranged and conducted by Dr. G. Child.

A most frightful tragedy occured during the evening of Sunday August 27, 1911. Hythe boatman Jack Godden left Hythe Pier bound for the Town Quay with three clients aboard, but his boat filled and sank when about 15 minutes out, almost in hailing distance of the Test Quays.
Three of the men including the boatman, died while the fourth man, Mr. Edwin Sloper, became a hero. When the boat sank being the only swimmer among the four, Mr. Sloper with another of his fellow passengers in tow made for the **Melissa**, a steamship lying at the Test Quay from which they were spotted in the water and quickly taken aboard. Mr. Slopers' colleague collapsed on being taken aboard and despite frantic attempts by the Ship's Doctor of the Royal Rotterdam Lloyd liner **Tambora**, lying at a adjacent berth, to revive him, he died.

Edwin Sloper was publicly recognised as a hero at the United Methodist Church, Eastleigh on November 8 where he was presented with a cheque for £5 on behalf of the Carnegie Hero Trust Fund.

At a meeting of the Southampton Harbour Board on October 5 a letter was read requesting "that the boats plying for hire from Hythe should be properly registered". A resolution was moved and carried "to reply, expressing regret at the (aforementioned) accident and to state that the matter is receiving the attention of the Board".

It might be noted that at this time Mr. T. Hoad was in charge of the Hythe Pier refreshment rooms. The **Hampton** went into the Northam yard of Messrs. Day, Summers & Co. for repair work to be carried out on August 27, 1912.

The 1912 Annual Hythe Regatta was held off the Pier on September 25 in fine, but cold, weather with an east-south-east wind blowing, which enabled the sailing programme to be completed in good time.

As usual the Hythe Yacht Club made premises available and decorated the Pier for the occasion. Among the yachts moored at or off the Pier were the **Lady Camilla**, the **Moonstone** and the **St. Joles**.

After the completion of the Regatta programme at about 6 o'clock there was music and dancing which lasted well into the evening, and needless to say, the steamers did an excellent day's business.

An accident causing injury to one of the Hythe Pier's porters, Wiliam Wyatt, happened on November 1. He was assisting to load some meat into a four wheeled van standing inside the Pier railings, when the horse attached to the van bolted. As the horse made it's way through the Pier gates a rear wheel caught and came away. Mr. Wyatt who was trying to stop the horse became trapped under the vehicle and was dragged a considerable distance. The horse was eventually stopped and Mr. Wyatt removed to his home for medical attention. Other than bruising and shock he was fortunately unhurt and able to return to work a few days later.

A Mr. H. Longlais of Marchwood applied to the Southampton Harbour Board during November 1912 for a licence to operate a motor boat between Cracknore Hard, the Town Quay and Hythe Pier, but was refused. The steamer services were badly affected by the weather again during the Winter of 1912/1913. It was most inclement on November 26 when the reward for a most hazardous walk along the very exposed Pier was an even greater ordeal on passage. On January 13 and February 11 dense fog limited the number of crossings during the mornings to but a few, while on the latter the programme was abandoned completely during the afternoon, leaving return ticket

Sailing barges Hythe Quay 1911. (Courtesy Theo Somes)

holders stranded in either Hythe or Southampton. On March 29, the Hampshire Independent recorded, "it is many years since the wind blew with such tremendous force as on Saturday" (March 22). The report went on, "about 8 o'clock in the evening a shelter box at one of the landing places on the Pier was blown clean away from it's position, and disappeared overboard. Those who went off to place the Hythe steamboat on her mooring for the night had all their work cut out to get ashore again".

A complaint was made by the Harbour Master to the Southampton Harbour Board on May 8, 1913 to the effect that the person in command of the Hythe steamer the previous day had disobeyed his instruction, depositing the steamer's passengers at the lower Town Quay landing steps and refusing to use the upper despite there being plenty of water. The incident was discussed and it was resolved to dispatch a letter to the captain of the Hythe steamers to the effect that should such an incident re-occur the Harbour Board would apply Sec. 53 of the Harbour, Docks and Pier Clauses Act 1847, which subjected any disregard of the Harbour Master's instructions to a fine of up to £20.

One of the Hythe steamers was engaged by Messrs. Morgan Giles and May, the Hythe yacht builders, on June 21 to provide a free excursion for their employees in celebration of the recent marriage of Mr. Morgan Giles. The party cruised about Southampton Water, watching the racing in a meeting of the Royal Southampton Yacht Club, and into the Hamble River where a crab tea was provided at Warsash. Hythe Pier was reached at about 8 o'clock after a very convivial and most successful outing.

A garden party was held on July 2 at a property in Hythe known as the Hard. Some 250 Southampton based persons attended the function. "The large company crossed in a special steamer, which was gaily decorated with flags and the ordinary boat". The Hythe and Dibden Conservative and Unionist Association chartered the **Hotspur** to make a return passage to Southampton so that 120 members could attend a public mass meeting at the Shirley Skating Rink on January 21, 1914 and listen to an

Going into The Marsh circa 1913.

address delivered by the Rt. Hon. J. Austen Chamberlain M.P. The excursion was an outstanding success and the party were safely disembarked at the Hythe Pier shortly before midnight.

A fierce gale blew throughout the day on February 12, 1914 and with an exceptionally high tide life was not easy for the steamers. All the passages were maintained, however, but not without injury. Several passengers lost hats and some suffered falls on the slippery decks of both the Pier and steamers. One of the Hythe Pier attendents, narrowly escaped injury while attending to the steamers ropes.

Twelve days later, on February 24, a passenger, aboard the steamer on passage drew the attention of the bridge to something in the water 500 yards to the Southampton side of Hythe Pier. On the steamer slowing up it was found to be a body, which was picked up and taken to Hythe.

The summer of 1914 came but with all apparently unaware of the political unrest in Europe that was to lead to the decaration of war on Germany on August 3 nothing was very different from any preceeding summer. Signor Marconi was a visitor to Hythe Pier on July 4 where he watched the starts of the yachting races of the Royal Southampton Yacht Club and was later joined by Sir Thomas Lipton who came ashore from the steam yacht **Erin** by launch.

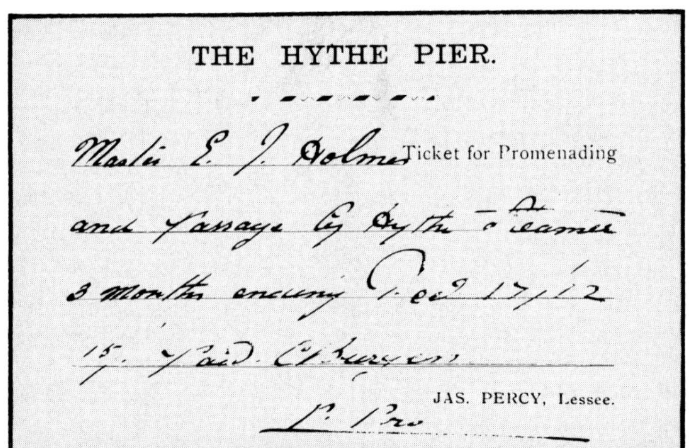

THE HYTHE PIER.

Master E. J. Holmes Ticket for Promenading

and Passage by Hythe Steamer

3 months ending Dec 17/12

15/- Paid.

JAS. PERCY, Lessee.

3 monthly Season Ticket issued September 1912.

War - Time Ferry Part One - August 1914 - November 1918

Colonel C. V. C. Hobart pictured in 1899 under the rank of Captain.

HAMPSHIRE INDEPENDENT, Saturday, August 1, 1914.

"A fortnight ago the political atmosphere of the Continent was, or appeared to be, serene and peaceful, and now suddenly the torch of war which has been thrown down by Austria threatens to set all Europe in a blaze. God grant that Great Britain will not be involved in the trouble".

War was declared on Germany at midnight on August 3.

The war was not going to be quickly won; that was so painfully obvious right from the start. Hythe quickly set about playing it's part in making it as short as possible. During August 1914, Mr. Maldwin Drummond, the recent successor to the Drummond Estate, put it's centre-piece, Cadland House, at the disposal of the authorities and the members of the Hythe Yacht Club at an emergency meeting held on the ninth instant resolved to make a similar gesture with regard to their Hythe Pier clubhouse. The latter immediately became the headquarters for Dr. Child's committee for organising assistance for the war effort. Lt. Col. C.V.C. Hobart offered his home at West Cliff Hall to the military authorities, who accepted and turned it into a Red Cross Hospital with accommodation for 25 persons.
The public, too, answered recruitment appeals; the Hythe Pier and Hythe and Southampton Ferry Company provided Lt. Col. Hobart and Mr. Arthur Lane to name but two. Lt. Col. Hobart, a director, was appointed to the Embarkation Staff at Southampton during October 1914, but fought in the field between November 1914 and February 1915 when he was appointed Railhead Commandant.
Mr. Arthur Lane, an engineer on the Hythe steamer, joined up during January 1916 and was detailed to one of the Royal Navy's requisitioned patrol boats.

Hampton and the 1911 White Star liner Olympic, (sister of the ill-fated Titanic), shortly prior to the outbreak of hostilities. (Courtesy Theo Somes)

Activity at Pier entrance early in the War, with Mr Kingham's additional sidings in use.

So far as can be ascertained no serious injury was inflicted upon any of the company's volunteers, although one director had a miraculous escape. Lord Montagu was a passenger aboard the s.s. **Persia** when she was torpedoed whilst on passage in the Mediterranean on December 30, 1915. Much concern was felt in both Hythe and even more so, Beaulieu. The Beaulieu Parish Magazine, February 1916, records,

> "The miraculous escape of Lord Montagu from the sinking of the **Persia** has filled our minds. On Sunday January 2 very earnest prayers were offered for his safety; and on the following Sunday most heartfelt thanksgivings was made. He arrived home on the 20th and has been warmly greeted by all his friends high and low".

Lord Montagu told the story of his escape in his paper "Car" shortly after arriving home. He wrote,

> "Two minutes after the explosion the deck was at such an angle that it was impossible to stand. I had just time, after going to my boat on the port side, and seeing that there was no chance of being saved on that side, to climb up to the starboard side, dragging with me my lady secretary, Miss Thornton".

He continued,

> "Hardly had I reached the starboard rail when the ship went rapidly down by the stern, and a huge wall of water engulfed me. I was sucked down by the vortex created by the sinking ship, and then blown up again by the returning water and escaping air and steam".

Lord Montagu on surfacing immediately made for a signal locker just suitable to support a single person. He was beaten to it, but was eventually able to cling to a boat, which unfortunately, was overturned several times causing the deaths of several of the occupants.

Back on local waters, the biggest impact felt as a result of the hostilities was what might appear somewhat surprising, a fantastic increase in volume of traffic. The Easter Bank Holiday of April 1915 was a fine day and a large number of passengers were taken across from Southampton to sample the delights of Hythe and the New Forest. "The single steamer service between here (Hythe) and Southampton was hardly sufficient to accommodate people anxious to get into the New Forest from Hythe and two extra trips had to be made by the steamer in order to cope with the passenger traffic in the evening." On Whit Monday 1915, (May 24), it was estimated that "some five or six thousand visited the village from Southampton," but this time "an extra steamer was put on in order to cope" and "additional turns beyond the advertised times were needed to get the people back to Southampton." On August 2, 1915 (Bank Holiday Monday), the morning traffic was even greater than that carried at Whitsuntide but by midday heavy rain had started to fall, so the traffic was all one way. On a fine, sunny September 12, 1915, a total of over 900 persons visited Hythe by steamer, a massive figure for an ordinary Sunday. The reason for the huge increase was threefold. Two reasons which added just a small number were the shortage of some commodities in Hythe shops which could usually be obtained form the markets and stores of Southampton and the ban on private fishing from boats, which meant anglers had to make for a structure projecting well from the shore as an alternative — Hythe Pier being one to gain additional revenue from this source. Reports of some fine whiting, bass and mullet being hauled ashore did much to promote the structure on this count. The main increase came as a result of the take-over by the military authorities of most of the Southampton Common during the early part of 1915. Hythe was still very green, and perfect for a deprived Southampton public.

During the early part of September 1915 the General Estates Company wrote to the Southampton Harbour Board seeking their approval of a plan to run the 40 foot motor launch **Hamble** in conjunction with or in the place of the **Hotspur** and/ or **Hampton**. The General Estates Company had acquired the 2 steamers from Mr. Percy (who was the Managing Director of this concern) on January 1, 1915. On September 23, the request was given Harbour Board approval subject to the findings of a Board of Trade survey on the launch. A certificate was granted by the Board of Trade and the **Hamble**, a vessel able to carry some 50—60 passengers, was first employed on the passage during October.

As in 1915, the Southampton public enjoyed the facilities offered at Hythe during 1916. On July 30 "there was a large influx of visitors to this side of the water from Southampton, and in the evening an extra trip had to be made by the steamer in order to get them all back again." On August 2 "there was quite a rush for the 3 o'clock steamer, which came over from Southampton quite full. It was most enjoyable along the shore from the village to Frost Lane and very many children enjoyed a paddle in the briney."

1917 followed a similar course with the numbers seemingly growing with each Bank Holiday. Easter Monday (April 1) 1918 was a busy day also, although one steamer supplemented by the **Hamble** managed to cope. Each Saturday and Sunday, the crowds continued the invasion and for Hythe, Whit Monday (May 20) 1918 was a day to remember. The Hampshire Independent (May 25) recorded,

> "Never since the institution of the Bank holiday has there been such an influx of visitors to the village as was the case on Whit Monday. Two steamboats had to be used in order to take the thousands who came over from Southampton during the day supplemented by the motor launch, and even then all those who wished to go to Hythe were unable to do so. The great difficulty was getting the people back to Southampton that evening and this was only accomplished by continuous passages to and fro, all being got over fortunately without mishap and in good time, although for the pushing and squeezing for a passage that prevailed at intervals there were one or two narrow escapes from a dip in the "briney". Those in charge of the steamers and others engaged in connection therewith had all their work cut out to prevent accidents and tact and judgement had to be displayed in dealing with the vast number of pleasure-seekers with whom Hythe and the district now seem to be a favourite resort and more especially at holiday times."

The holiday and week-end traffic was by this time far in excess of the combined capacity of the **Hotspur**, the **Hampton** and the **Hamble**. On week-days, too, each crossing was well filled. So that the prospective traffic could receive the service it was seeking, the General Estates Company transferred the screw steamer **Southtown** from the Yarmouth — Gorleston service. The **Southtown** arrived at Hythe from Yarmouth on September 29, 1918 and it was the intention to place her on the passage as soon as the required Board of Trade survey was carried out. She was "a screw steamer some 10 feet longer than either of the old boats and very nicely fitted up below".

It was announced at about this time by the

Pier approach circa 1916.

Southtown, which arrived at Hythe in 1918, pictured at Great Yarmouth in 1930

General Estates Company that further vessels were being sought, including "a twin screw launch capable of carrying 150 passengers". A contemporary reporter, on this announcement, recalled the days when "the communications between Hythe and Southampton was kept up by licenced watermen with sailing wherries and rowing boats and when the landing at Hythe was on the old Hard." "We think," continued the reporter, "there is only one waterman left who "plied the ferry" in the old days and he is Richard Edwards of Southampton who can relate some very interesting yarns of this experience."

The General Estates Company were genuinely looking forward in earnest to providing the people of Hythe, and Southampton too, the best facilities they had ever known. Backtracking just a little, the General Estates Company published their 1917 Winter programme as follows:—

SOUTHAMPTON AND HYTHE FERRY
TIME TABLE FOR WINTER SERVICE
ALL FARES INCLUDE HYTHE PIER TOLL

Single Fares - 1st Class 9d. - 2nd Class 6d.
Return Fares - 1st Class 1/- - 2nd Class 9d.
Soldiers, Nurses, etc. - 1st Class 9d. - 2nd Class 6d. return.

A Boat will leave as under, weather and circumstances permitting.

FROM HYTHE		FROM SOUTHAMPTON	
Weekdays	Sundays	Weekdays	Sundays
5.15 a.m.		5.45 a.m.	
6.15 a.m.		6.45 a.m.	
8.0 a.m.		8.30 a.m.	
9.0 a.m.		9.30 a.m.	10.30 a.m.
10.0 a.m.	10.0 a.m.	10.30 a.m.	
11.0 a.m.	11.30 a.m.	11.30 a.m.	12.15 p.m.
12.0 a.m.		12.30 p.m.	2.0 p.m.
1.10 p.m.	1.30 p.m.	2.0 p.m.	3.0 p.m.
2.30 p.m.	2.30 p.m.	3.0 p.m.	4.0 p.m.
3.30 p.m.	3.30 p.m.	4.0 p.m.	5.30 p.m.
4.30 p.m.	5.0 p.m.	5.0 p.m.	
5.30 p.m.		6.0 p.m.	
6.30 p.m.		7.0 p.m.	
7.30 p.m.		8.0 p.m.	
8.30 p.m.*		9.15 p.m.*	

* Saturdays only

Second Class Tickets only, available for any part of the Boat, will be issued on Sundays.
Proprietors:
THE GENERAL ESTATES CO. LTD.
Manager:
J.R. ROBERTS, Pier Office, Hythe.

There were plenty of problems resulting from inclement weather, too. A violent gale blew across the neighbourhood during the evening and night of December 28, 1914. At the height of the winds the **Hotspur** set out to make a passage to Southampton. She was skillfully manouvered along the Dibden shoreline, well to windward, and reached the Town Quay safely. Her passengers were subjected to a very bouncy crossing all the same but had some compensation in witnessing the spectacular sight of the waves clearing the well illuminated Southampton Docks sheds. The weather over Christmas 1915 was "very boisterous" and "consequently the steam boat traffic was not as large as usual."
"The passage was very rough, big seas sweeping over the steamer at intervals, but she was able to keep up the service with great punctuality, all things considered."

Intending passengers were not so lucky on November 5, 1916, however. All morning passages were cancelled as the wind at times reached hurricane force. One or two crossings were managed during the afternoon when the wind, albeit still very strong, lulled a little. Landing at both Hythe Pier and the Town Quay was very perilous as the water was being whipped up and sent crashing over both Hythe Pier and the Southampton Harbour Board offices at the Town Quay. The passenger traffic was even more inconvenienced, on November 17, 1916 when a south-easterly gale "of considerable violence" prevented the crewmen, despite several attempts, to even get the steamer away from her moorings and alongside Hythe Pier. Had they managed that "it would have been absolutely dangerous for the vessel to have "put to sea" and so the day's programme was abandoned early on. This was perhaps the worst possible day, being a Friday and "market day", for such an inconvenience. Many people, not only from

Hythe but Fawley, Dibden and Beaulieu too, used the facilities provided by the steamers to fetch their week-end provisions.

The carriers who ran goods brought over by the steamer from Hythe Pier to the customers in Fawley, Beaulieu and along the way were badly affected. A party including in their number Sir Robert Hobart arrived at the Town Quay en route from London to Hythe but had to complete their journey by rail to Totton and carriage to Hythe. A concert party was due to entertain the wounded soldiers at West Cliff Hall, but could get no further than the Town Quay. Out of the confusion perhaps some of the people then complaining about the cost of voyaging across the passage might have realised exactly what they were getting for their fare.

Fog, too, had it's effect. It "greatly interfered with the ferry steamer traffic" on December 18, 1916 "as during the greater part of the day the steamer did not run". A very dense fog descended over Southampton Water on October 2, 1917 and prevented the operating of the early departure, at 5.45 a.m., from Southampton which had been introduced the previous April to bring over the workmen who were employed by Messrs. Jenkins and Sons of Southampton on the construction of new sheds in the Hythe shipyard of Messrs. May, Harden and May. The early part of the ordinary time-table was also cancelled, but at 10 o'clock Harry Banks took out his first command of the day.

The passage from Hythe Pier to the Town Quay was made at almost "dead slow" with the return journey not that much faster. The sun eventually broke through during the early afternoon but not until after Hythe Pier had survived a few moments of breathtaking anxiety. With the density of the fog at it's height a steamer was converging on Hythe Pier apparently quite unaware of the structure. Fortunately one of the pier attendents, Mr. T. Diaper, saw the vessel through the gloom and hailed of the danger. With her engines at "full speed astern" she managed to clear the Pier by just a couple of yards and avoid a collision that might have had serious consequences.

As well as providing better facilities for the increasing traffic by introducing the **Hamble** and the **Southtown** during the war years the General Estates Company had the **Hampton** and later the **Hotspur** made more comfortable in having them equipped with electric lighting. Mr. James Percy arranged for the **Hampton** to undergo this operation when he withdrew her from service in December 1914. She re-appeared on the passage, replacing the **Hotspur**, during mid April, 1915 after a 5 months lay-off during which not only was the new lighting installed but much essential repair work and modernisation carried out. Smokey old oil lamps were abandoned to the relief of the passengers who spent many a journey in total darkness on a windy night.

On August 26, 1915 the sailing barge **Itchen** came into collision with Hythe Pier. She lost her topmast, but fortunately didn't damage the Pier.

The Hythe steamer was visited by the local constabulary involved in the search for three missing boys, during the morning of May 11, 1916. The boys, Reggie (aged 11 years), Norman (9) and Cecil (7) Spray were sent out from their Southampton home at 8.00 a.m. the previous day to do some shopping, being given 2s 4d for the task by their parents. The boys were very late returning, and the police informed. Reports came quickly to the Southampton police that three boys answering the descriptions given were seen on board the steamer during the day (May 10) and in Hythe during the evening. Their journey there was unexplainable, but another sighting was reported by a postman at Bramshot Hill, Dibden during the early morning of May 11. The search in and around Hythe continued for a number of days thereafter until reports reached Southampton that they had been found wandering in Oxford Street, London.

After 5 days of walking and sleeping on the roadside they were safely returned to their anxious parents. A touch of pathos just for the record, Cecil said,

> "we did not forget to say our prayers, mummy and every night we knelt down and asked God to protect us and forgive us for going away".

It has already been recorded that certain commodities were often short in the Hythe shops, but one thing that wasn't short during June 1918 was butcher's meat. Petrol being very scarce, the steamer was requisitioned to carry over the passage much of the supplies needed to keep the shops of Hythe stocked. A "good consignment of beef" came across from Southampton on the 3 o'clock steamer during the afternoon of May 31. Another "large quantity" was conveyed during the afternoon of June 25, the unloading of which "occupied a considerable time" "detaining the steamer quite half-an-hour". The premises vacated by the Hythe Yacht Club, who incidently had suspended operations during May 1915 for the duration of hostilities, was being used as a temporary warehouse for the cargoes carried by the steamer, but only for the short period of time needed to sort out individual requirements.

The steamer was suggested as defence evidence, by the defendents in two separate cases heard by the Hythe Petty Sessions towards the end of the war. The first, came before the court on October 25, 1917. The defendant was summoned for riding his bicycle after lighting-up time with neither a front nor a rear lamp. He claimed that because of the breakdown of the Hythe steamer he had been detained in the village, but the prosecution policeman repudiated the claim informing the Bench that the failure of the steamer had not affected the time-table as the launch **Hamble** had been speedily requisitioned.

On August 8, 1918 a second defendant answering a charge of being drunk and disorderly the previous day, claimed that although he had had a "drop" of whisky in Southampton and two glasses of bitter in Hythe, it was "crossing the water" that had "upset him".

War-time obituary columns were unusually long but included among them were very few who had at some time featured in the story of the Hythe Ferry.

Unquestionably the most regretable was that of Mr. James Percy on May 17, 1915. Mr. Percy first became associated with the Hythe Ferry when he tendered for the Hythe Pier tolls in January 1887, following Mr. Frederick Fry's refusal to partake in such an auction. Mr. Percy, already experienced as a lessee of tolls and steamboat proprietor, put in a bid of £665 per annum and was offered the position on a three year term on February 7, 1887. He acquired the steamboats then plying the passage, the **Louisa** and the **Frederica**, from Mr. Fry on March 2 at a further cost of £475. He obviously realised the potential of the Hythe-Southampton passage as by the following February (1888) he had placed an order for a new steamer from Messrs. Willoughby Bros. of Plymouth. The **Hotspur**, as the new vessel was appropriately christened, took her station in April 1889 and was joined

James Percy pictured in 1913

by a second new steamer, the **Hampton**, in May 1894. Mr. Percy operated the **Hotspur** and the **Hampton** very successfully and had a bonus during the early war years of having to acquire the **Hamble** to be able to cope with the volume of traffic.

Age was creeping on, so on January 1, 1915 he sold his steamers to the General Estates Co. Ltd., the London based family firm which dated back to 1900 and of which he was the Managing Director. In his eighty-second year he died at his home, Hotspur Lodge, Ealing Common, London. His personal fortune amounted to £52,813, the main executors of which were his widow, Mrs. Emma Percy, and Messrs. William Herbert Percy, who was to succeed to the head of the family business, and Thomas Bernard Percy.

Mr. W.H. Percy pledged to develop the traffic and immediately set about keeping up the good will built up by his predecessor. This gentleman acquired local headquarters during the afternoon of May 11, 1917, when he successfully put in the highest bid for a pair of cottages known as Nos. 1 and 2, The Grove, Hythe. The properties which were acquired at an auction at the Dolphin Hotel, Southampton and said to be the place where Oliver Cromwell slept when he visited Southampton, cost Mr. W.H. Percy the sum of £680.

An armistice was signed on November 11, 1918. "On Monday" (November 11, 1918) "there were great rejoicings at Hythe". "Flags were displayed in all parts of the village, and work was suspended at the large establishments in the place where the utmost enthusiasm prevailed throughout the day".

'Tween The Wars

December 1918, the War was over; the victory celebrations complete; the task of restoring Hythe's pre-war serene and tranquil air was under way.

Sadly it wasn't to be the Hythe of old. Within the comparitively short time of only seven years, massive tracts of the Drummond Estate were sold off as development land to the AGWI Oil Company, the long talked about railway eventually arrived, new roads and the widening of many of the lanes was necessary for the motor car, by this time not only a privilege of the well to do, and for the Hythe Ferry — a new business-like approach to replace the familiarity between owner and passenger that seemingly died along with Mr. James Percy. This statement is not meant to take anything whatsoever away from the General Estates Company, who acquired the ferry steamers from Mr. Percy back in 1915 and gradually procured the shares owned by local people in the Hythe Pier and Hythe and Southampton Ferry Company during the early 1920's, when the first of the directors of the General Estates Company sought election to the Board of the Hythe Pier and Hythe and Southampton Ferry Company which, incidently, shortened it's name to a more manageable title, the Hythe Pier Company Ltd., in 1923. The General Estates Company's intentions were honourable, but somehow the people of Hythe time after time found cause for complaint — the methods, the service, the fares and so on. Perhaps, as with the early promotors of the passage, their alien headquarters left them somewhat distant from a very vexed traffic.

Not everybody, by any means, was disenchanted with the General Estates Company during the early years after the war. One group of people who took quite a different view was their employees for whom a dinner was laid on, on Boxing Day, 1918. So that nobody would miss out on the proceedings the scheduled service was abandoned at 6.00 p.m. This concession was much appreciated by the 30 employees and their partners.

New Road and St. John's Street at the end of the war.

At an assembly of a local group known as the Progressive Association on May 6, 1919, the meeting, adopted a resolution "for the Association to approach the Ferry Company to see whether it would be possible to run a ferry on Wednesday and Saturday nights leaving Southampton at 10.30 p.m. in order to enable the residents to visit a theatre or other places of amusement." During the course of the next few months, this group had the question of local communications on it's agenda several times. Regarding the Hythe Ferry, representatives were in touch with the owners of both the Hythe Pier and the Hythe steamers. At a meeting on April 13, 1920, it was reported that the owners of Hythe Pier were in the process of carrying out repairs as deemed necessary by the group's representatives and were about to introduce an electric tram while the owners of the steamers had promised a much improved service for the fast approaching Summer months. The Dibden Parish Council too, were not entirely satisfied with the General Estates Company's time-table for in a meeting on March 29, 1920 it was minuted that "a plea was put in for a better boat service between Southampton and Hythe with a not very confident hope that this would be accompanied by a reduction of fares." The fares at this time being 6d single and 9d return.

Away from these arguments, life returned to normal. On (Whit Monday) May 24, 1920 "a very large number of people took a trip across to Hythe" "under ideal conditions." "The South shore-road was crowded with pic-nic parties and presented a truly sea-side scene." The General Estates Company expanded on their business of operating the Hythe passage by offering "Steam Trips to the Hamble River" and the "Hire of Motor Boats for Pleasure and Fishing." On Hythe Pier, itself, the YMCA were renting the former clubhouse of the Hythe Yacht Club as the latter had not taken up it's option at the end of the war. It had been hoped to form a "Red Triangle Sailing Club" but by agreement with the Pier owners a public refreshment room was fitted out and opened on June 30, 1919 "for the benefit of all those who wish to use Hythe Pier."

The Hythe Pier Regatta not staged since the Summer of 1913 was revived on August 21, 1920 with a new title, the Hythe and Dibden Regatta. Although cold, a large crowd gathered on Hythe Pier to witness the first race scheduled for a 10.00 a.m. start and a varied selection of fine music was presented by the Beaulieu Brass Band during the afternoon and evening.

The improvement of the steamer service for the summer months of 1920 was short-lived as by mid October all evening passages after 6.00 p.m. had been cancelled. This move presented additional ammunition for the campaign for a better service, particularly as each of the steamers had long since been equipped with electric lighting. An amusing incident arose from the introduction of the Winter time-table when on October 27 an

The Yarmouth pictured at Great Yarmouth, September 1930.

attendant through force of habit rang out the toll bell for the 6.30 p.m. departure from Hythe Pier, quite forgetting the steamer was already on her moorings. It was announced in the local press on December 18, 1920 that the **Hampton** was about to be replaced back on the passage to relieve the **Yarmouth**. So far as can be traced this has been the only reference to a Hythe ferry-boat named **Yarmouth**. "The inhabitants of Hythe and district will welcome the news" wrote the reporter.

During February 1921 the Royal Motor Yacht Club occupied the premises formerly rented by the Hythe Yacht Club and subsequently the YMCA on Hythe Pier. The former two organisations had amalgamated for the benefit of local yachtsmen but the pact was not to last too long as within the matter of just a few months the Hythe Yacht Club was to be re-constituted to operate from premises off the Hythe shipyards.

During the early part of 1921 the question of the light railway between Totton and Fawley was raised once again. Prior to a public enquiry arranged to be held at the Oddfellows Hall, Hythe on May 11, the Dibden Parish Council included the matter on their agenda for a meeting on April 12. The purpose was to decide upon the nature of their opposition. As the schedule did not mention a station at Hythe it was the opinion of several of the councillors that the promoters, viz the AGWI Oil Company and the London and South Western Railway Company who had acquired an order back in 1903, but had not carried it through, were primarily interested in such a line for the conveyance of goods. After considerable discussion, it was resolved that the Dibden Parish Council would not be in favour of the scheme unless it was to serve the passengers and goods of Hythe and district and not just, as it would appear, the private enterprise at Fawley. The public enquiry granted the application after the

The Shipyard, Hythe, early twenties.

promoters had agreed to an additional station along the line, at Hythe. Unlike previous applications for the line, there was no opposition offered by either the Hythe Pier and Hythe and Southampton Ferry Company or the General Estates Company. Perhaps for the latter it was as well that there wasn't bearing in mind the criticism circulating at the time. Work was to commence during the Autumn of 1923.

The General Estates Company's misery continued. The Hampshire Independent published on November 11, 1921, a letter from a "Reader".

> "I had occasion to go over to Hythe one evening last week by the 7 p.m. boat. Directly we left the Quay all lights were put out, and the whole deck was plunged into darkness. Lately there have been no rumours of submarines in Southampton Water, and one can only conclude that it must be on the grounds of economy, and not on those of safety. Many of the passengers would like to read during the journey over, and I think it would be greatly appreciated by them if the Company would see their way clear to light the decks."

January 3, 1922 was a very sad day for the Hythe passage. A tragic accident occured resulting in the death of one of the Hythe ferry crewmen, Henry Diaper. It would appear, although nobody really knew, that Mr. Diaper fell into the water while attempting to climb aboard the **Hampton** from a rowing boat to perform the early morning duties that were for him an everyday task. His body was found on the mud later in the day during a search which was put into action as soon as the unmanned boat was observed floating off the pier.

The Royal Motor Yacht Club premises on Hythe Pier were extensively modernised in time for the 1922 racing season. On March 18 it was announced that "comfortable and roomy quarters are now available, including a large dining room, galley, bar, and four sleeping cabins. There is besides, a bath-room."

Shore Road circa 1920.

A Dibden Parish Council meeting on May 15, 1922 had the Hythe Ferry up for discussion, once again. This time to discuss a protest about the additional amount above the advertised fare being taxed on those buying tickets once on board the steamer after having failed to do so at Hythe tollhouse. Sir Robert Hobart, a former director of the Hythe Pier and Hythe and Southampton Ferry Company, urged a Board of Trade enquiry. After a lengthy speech in which Lt. Col. C.V.C. Hobart told the history of the Hythe Ferry, the Hythe Pier and the old Hythe Hard and further made it known that there was nothing to prevent competition on the passage, a resolution was carried "that the Parish Council should be asked to call a special public meeting of the travelling public of Hythe and surrounding districts with a view to demanding a Board of Trade enquiry into the methods of the Hythe and Southampton Steam Ferry Company."

On the credit side the General Estates Company put on "a special boat" from Hythe Pier at 10.00 p.m. on September 27, 1922 so that those attending the Hythe Oddfellows meeting at the St. John's Hall, Hythe could return to Southampton. And, during July, an electric tramway had been introduced onto Hythe Pier, a facility which was perhaps the biggest boon to the travelling public since the construction of Hythe Pier itself back in 1879—1880. Three locomotives, of Brush construction, were acquired, one of which has since been dismantled to provide spares for the other two. They had been built during the Great War for use in the Avonmouth Mustard Gas Factory where they were battery operated at 100 volts. At Hythe the batteries were removed and the locomotives fitted up with collector shoes. Operating at 200 volts (subsequently 240 volts), the tramway collected it's power from a third rail laid on the south side of the track which itself was laid on the south side of the pier away from that put down by Mr. Kingham's workmen in 1909, on the northern side. It was fed by a small generating station, which also supplied the village, near the tollhouse. Passenger carrying rolling stock consisting of three two-bogie unsprung carriages built by the Drewry Car Company Ltd. carried up to 48 persons along the Pier three minutes prior to each ferry departure. The General Estates Company operated the tramway, painted out green and cream and sporting in black shaded letters on the carriage doors the initials "HPR", under lease in accordance with the 1878 Hythe Pier Order.

One of the earliest pictures of the Hythe Pier train, this 1922 Mudge photograph also shows the motor launch Hamble.

As suggested by Sir Robert Hobart and resolved by the Dibden Parish Council the previous May, official representations were made during the early months of 1923. As a result the following correspondence passed between the Ministry of Transport and the renamed Hythe Pier Company Ltd.

Ministry of Transport,
Secretarial and Legal Dept.,
6, Whitehall Gardens
London S.W.1.

Sir,

I am directed by the Minister of Transport to state for the information of the Hythe Pier and Hythe and Southampton Ferry Co. Ltd., that representations have recently been made to him regarding the facilities provided at Hythe Pier.

The Minister is informed that of the five pier landings originally provided for the public two were removed some years ago, and two are now being removed, with the result that it is impossible to land from a boat except at the extreme end of the pier.

It is stated that the pier is used largely by the public desiring to catch the ferry boat to Southampton, and that when the

Pier Tramway is not running it is necessary to walk the whole length of the pier, a distance of about 800 yards, along which no shelter is provided against bad weather.

Complaint has also been made that on at least two occasions persons were refused tickets for the tramway.

The Minister would be glad to be furnished with the observations of the Company on these representations.

I am, Sir,
Your obedient servant,
(signed) R.H. Hill

The reply of the Hythe Pier Company Ltd.,

Sir,

My directors instruct me to state in reply to yours of the 19th. ulto. that although contrary to the usual practise, you do not state the source of the representations recently made to the Ministry of Transport regarding the facilities provided at Hythe Pier, they assume that the Minister of Transport is satisfied that such source is sufficiently responsible to warrant, in the general interest of the public, his detailed consideration of the three representations, which otherwise might have appeared to be of a somewhat frivolous description.

1. My directors are not aware of the precise nature of the landings originally provided, the pier having been constructed about 45 years ago. The intermediate landings mentioned are not part of the original structure. In addition to the low water landing at the extreme end of the pier, a wharf and hard are provided which are available for landing at other states of the tide.

2. Persons walking along the Pier are naturally exposed to the weather, as is the case of practically all piers. There are shelters at each end.

3. An electric tram service, provided and operated in conjunction with the steam ferry service to the Town Quay, Southampton, started working in July last, a development which is of considerable benefit to and much appreciated by the residents in the locality. This company does not own or operate either the electric trams or the ferry steamers, but has enquired as to the apparently absurd allegation that persons have been refused tram tickets, and it may be noted that neither dates, times, names or any other circumstances are mentioned. Possibly this representation relates to a case where persons, late for steamer, have wished to have a tram run specially for their convenience and the steamer detained, to enable them to catch it. On no occasion has any person been prevented from taking any seat not otherwise occupied in the tram about to start.

I am, Sir,
Your obedient servant,
(signed) P. HARRIS, Secretary.

During July 1924 Jones Lane and New Road were closed to traffic to allow bridge construction as the laying of the railway track was fast approaching Hythe. The manner in which the contractors were leaving their plant caused great inconvenience and on occasions caused persons sufficient delay to miss the steamer, on one occasion the last one of the day. The General Estates Company approached the Dibden Parish Council to keep such obstruction to it's absolute minimum.

The Summer of 1925 saw the opening of the Totton to Fawley railway, first proposed some 45 years previous. Until this time the Hythe passage had only an uninspiring omnibus service for competition, but July 19 saw the first passenger train along the line.

New competition for the General Estates Company as the first train along the new railway line arrives at Fawley Station.

On May 22, 1926, it was announced that an order had been placed by the General Estates Company for a new semi-Diesel engined ferry "to supplement the present ferry service." A party from Hythe, including among it's number Messrs. T.B. Percy (by this time Managing Director of the General Estates Company), J.D. Percy, J.R. Roberts (Manager) and A. Lane (Foreman at Hythe), arrived at Cowes during the morning of January 17, 1927 for the launching of the new vessel. She was of a flush deck type, designed by her builders, Messrs. J. Samuel White & Co.

Mrs. Percy, Wife of Mr. T.B. Percy, performed the ceremony with the words,

> "I name you **Hotspur** and wish you every success."

At the end of March the General Estates Company applied to the Board of Trade for permission to change the name of the old **Hotspur** (of 1889), to **G.E.C.**, so that a duplication of names could be avoided as the new **Hotspur** was about to be delivered. On Easter Monday, April 18, 1927 the new **Hotspur** was put into commission, while the old **Hotspur**, renamed **G.E.C.**, made way into obscurity. Very little is on record for the first years of retirement for the **G.E.C.**, until that is, the following advertisement appeared in the local press on July 20, 1929.

STEAMBOAT FOR SALE
The original "Hotspur" Hythe Ferry Boat (now renamed G.E.C.).
Price £450, new boiler in 1922.
Seen at Hythe Pier.
G.E.C., 20, Bond Street,
Ealing, London.

Although the advertisement was repeated weekly until September 7, enquiries were few and definite offers none at all. The original **Hotspur**, after 38 years of

The first Hotspur (of 1889) pictured here on January 16, 1927 awaits her fate as....

.... a new Hotspur takes to the water the following day.

stalwart service, was made to suffer the ignominy of being stripped of her engine, boiler and anything else that might have had some spare part value and towed into Dibden Bay to be left at the mercy of the elements; eventually rusting away.

cause an obstruction to steam vessels using the port, contrary to the bye-laws of the Harbour Board." The case arose as their yachts, the **Gweno**(Miss Hobart), the **Julia** (Mr. Roberts) and the **Fancy Free** (Mr. Banks), taking part in a race across

Still waiting, the 1889 Hotspur, renamed GEC, under offer in 1928.

The racing of the Royal Motor Yacht Club and the Hythe Sailing Club from their headquarters at Hythe Pier and the Hythe shipyards respectively, was a feature of the Hythe Summer scene. Although more often than not very "run of the mill" there was occasional incident. Such was the case on June 18, 1927 when one race in the Hythe Sailing Club programme didn't go exactly to plan and led to three of the participants appearing at the Southampton Police Court on July 26. The three persons, Miss Irene Hobart of Langdown House, Hythe, (daughter of Sir Robert Hobart), Mr. J. R. Roberts of The Grove, Hythe and Manager of the General Estates Company and Mr. Edward James Banks also of Hythe, were all summoned by the Southampton Harbour Board for "making use of the deep water channel in Southampton Water in such a way as to

the deep water channel, ran across the bows of the tanker **British Grenadier**. For fear of running down the yachts the pilot aboard the tanker which was moving up-river, ordered the vessel full astern. As a result of his action his command almost came into contact with another yacht, the **Magdalene**. Tugs were needed to straighten up the tanker and while doing so the steam-ships **Pennland** and **Alaunia** had to be detained in port.

Each of the defendents, pleaded not guilty but the Bench saw the verdict in favour of the Southampton Harbour Board, imposing the maximum fine of £5.

On August 9, 1927, sponsored by the Southampton Amateur Swimming Club, 20 members and two visitors to Hythe took to the water to swim from Hythe Pier to Southampton's Royal Pier. The swimmers, only five of whom failed to finish the course, took a course in choppy conditions along the Marchwood side of the river until parallel to the Town Quay where a change of direction towards the Royal Pier was required. A large crowd assembled on the Royal Pier to greet the swimmers, some of whom had also watched them leave Hythe Pier, travelling across by steamer.

The next half-dozen years or so were very ordinary years so far as affairs both on and off the Hythe passage were concerned. Sadly, however, several deaths of persons who have featured in the story of the Hythe Ferry to date occured, including Sir Robert Hobart, and Lord Montagu. The earliest was that of Sir Robert Hobart on August 4, 1928, who died peacefully at Langdown House at the age of 91. He was educated at Charterhouse and Trinity Hall, Cambridge and entered Civil Service in 1860, retiring in 1900. In 1901 he was selected to act as secretary for the coronation of King Edward VII. He represented the New Forest in the House of Commons between 1906 and 1910, under Liberal Party colours. He was made a C.B. in 1884, a K.C.V.O. in 1901 and a Baronet in 1914. His heir to the latter was his son, Lt. Col. C.V.C. Hobart, who adopted the title Sir Vere Hobart.

Sir Robert married in 1869 and produced two children, a son, Claud Vere Cavendish, and a daughter, Irene. Sir Robert's connection with the Hythe Ferry dates back to the formation of the Hythe Pier and Hythe and Southampton Ferry Company in December 1874 when he was one of the founder directors. However, when the company was re-constituted towards the end of 1878 following their failure to comply with the conditions set out in the 1875 Hythe Pier Order, Sir Robert was nothing more than a shareholder. He was re-elected to the

Board of Directors on September 24, 1881 and served continuously for many years, exactly how many, however, is not certain.

Another former director of the Hythe Pier and Hythe and Southampton Ferry Company, Lord Montagu, the former Hon. J. Scott-Montagu, died on March 30, 1929.

Lord Montagu was born in 1866 the first son of Lord Henry Scott, the First Baron Montagu whom he was to succeed in 1905. His heir and the third and present Baron Montagu, Edward J.B. Douglas-Scott, was born in 1926.

Lord Montagu will be best remembered for his love of the motor car, he inaugerated a paper, "Car," devoted to it. Regarding the Hythe Ferry he joined his father on the Board of Directors of the Hythe Pier and Hythe and Southampton Ferry Company during the mid 1890's, serving for many years although as in the case of Sir Robert Hobart exactly how many is not certain.

During early thirties the editor of the Hampshire Advertiser appears to have had an obsession with features. Hythe and/or the ferry was included no less than five times during these years and twice more by the first publication of 1937. The first appeared under the title of "Autumn Hike" by "The Tramp" on September 12, 1931. For this hike "from Hythe to Brockenhurst by way of Beaulieu" wrote "The Tramp" "the starting place is Hythe, which can be reached from Southampton by ferry steamer from the Town Quay or by rail."

The second, entitled "Queer Things About Hythe" by G.H.S., appeared on March 24, 1934. "Hythe has been connected with Southampton by a steamboat ferry for as long as anyone in the village can remember," the author recorded, "but early in the nineteenth century the line of communication was maintained by a fleet of sailing wherries. The licenced wherrymen of Hythe were real characters such as Dickens would have enjoyed describing." The author proceeded to recall some of the wherrymen, men like Edward Banks and his wherry the **Canary**, John Banks (**Flying Cloud**), Harry Blanchard (**Deledern**), James Bratcher (**Gentle**), Harry Diaper (**Mary Ann**), "Slit" Randall (**Gundruna**), Henry Stephens (**Swift**) and Edward Wall (**Nora**). The first of the wherries, "long pointed boats with two masts," used to leave Hythe at about 5 o'clock each morning "with tradesmen and women folk who at this early hour were setting out to buy provisions in the markets of Southampton."

South Street during late twenties showing railway bridge built in 1924.

The third and fourth of these articles appeared in an Angling series by "Greenheart". "Greenheart's" first article, headed "Bank Holiday Fishing — A Day on Hythe Pier" was published on May 26, 1934.

"In view of the Whitsun holiday," he wrote, "it was somewhat difficult to form a boating party, and, this being so, I thought I would try my luck on Hythe Pier. Why is it when one mentions Hythe to a salt water angler he almost invariably laughs."

After relating his experiences of two previous fishing sessions on the pier "Greenheart" went on to tell of that of Whit Monday.

"Taking the first boat, 10.30., I found several anglers fishing from the pontoon on arrival; several others travelled in the same boat and proceeded to do so likewise, i.e. fish from the pontoon. When I walked up the pier for about a third of it's distance towards the shore, I expect they thought, 'let him go, poor fool, there will be all the more for us.' I went where I did because I knew I stood a good chance with the tide coming in of getting a few flounders in the shallow water; possibly some again on high water and again on the run out. I was not disappointed."

He continued,

"During the afternoon I heard from a passerby that about a dozen anglers on the end of the pier had nothing between them."

"On another occasion I returned to the water a fish of three or four ounces which was only lip hooked, and a young fellow standing by remarked: "They keep them that size where I come from"

"To cut a long story short," conlcluded "Greenheart", "I finished the day with eleven fish and returned four. Five of the fish were ¾lb or over, two of ½lb each and the remaining four would go about a pound the lot. I did not stop to fish the run off or no doubt I should have got several more fish."

"Greenheart" returned to Hythe Pier again on June 3, 1934 to report upon the second stage of a six event series for the H.E. Smith Cup fished for by the Southampton Sea Anglers Club. Mr. H.E. Smith, donor of the trophy, was also present. In his article on June 9 "Greenheart" told a yarn that must go down on record as the best of the "one that got away" stories.

"Early in the day he (a contestant) had landed a fish which was nearly an inch over the minimum length, but by the time weighing-in arrived this fish had behaved somewhat in the way of an Egyptian mummy and had shrunk to such an extent that when it reached the weighing-in table it was rejected by the stewards as being under-sized."

The fifth feature was one entitled "The Last of the Wherrymen" published on August 3, 1935. The Advertiser's reporter wrote that when he had asked one of the Southampton Harbour Board officials whether there were "any longshoremen to be found near the Town Quay these days" he received only a solemn look and a shake of the head.

"The story of the longshoreman is a sad one," came the reply after a few moments deliberation, "if you are thinking of breezy old salts in weather beaten guernseys and top boots, as ready to spin a yarn of sailing ship days over a pint of ale as to ferry you across the river — the sort of men you imagine at Wapping Wharf after reading Jacobs — then I'm afraid you'll be disappointed. In fact there are none left. The licenced waterman of today is a river taxi-driver — a mechanic who owns a motor boat. And he is not in the longshoreman tradition. But just a moment......"

Another few moments deliberation conjured up the name "Roper" Zebedee. Henry Zebedee, better known to his friends and colleagues for more than 60 years as "Roper" was the only survivor of the only

Thomas Bernard Percy who succeeded to the head of the General Estates Co. in the early 20's pictured in 1930.

High Street during early 1930's.

Hollybank House circa 1930.

survivor of the Southampton wherrymen. In his eightieth year he was living in Southampton after having retired only five years earlier.

"I've been about these waters for more than 60 years," recalled Mr. Zebedee, obviously enjoying reliving some of the moments of a colourful career, "so long in fact, that all the other wherrymen I worked with are dead. Some folk, I suppose, will remember their names ...... Richard Edwards, Harry (Henry) Hall, "Shallow" Edwards (we all had nicknames), Jack Low ...... there were many more but I can't rightly mind 'em just now. The business began to die, as you might say, 20 years ago or more. The wherrymen didn't buy new boats because, with falling business they couldn't afford them, and now there are none to be seen."

"But one day's time we were busy. I remember when I worked two days and nights at a stretch — not a moment for bed — we were that rushed. Besides taking passengers to Hythe and Cracknorehard, we used to take all the stores down to the yachts. Sometimes I used to hide myself away in the "Waterman's Arms" for an hour, so that I shouldn't be hired. When the last Hythe steamer sailed at half past five on winter afternoons, passengers off trains would sail across with us, and we had some rough passages I can tell you. I can remember how one baled the water out with his hard hat."

He continued to relate more of his experiences and included one or two interesting observations. He recalled that,

"most of the wherrymen had learnt their trade on sailing ships, and could tell good yarns of an evening of their experiences on board and in foreign ports."

And that,

"I (himself) once owned half a dozen wherries. We couldn't charge what we

Hollybank villas under construction in 1930.

liked, of course. There was a proper tariff which we all had to observe."

And finally,

"The wherries were built locally — in the yards along the Western Shore, almost opposite the entrance to the New Docks. I can well remember Stevens, Picket's and Moon's."

An article published on April 11, 1936 discussed the mood prevailing in Hythe at the time. Hythe, it said, was enjoying a "wave of prosperity." Nothing could have been more true. Of the approximate working population of 1,800 (including that of Fawley), only 64 were "on the dole." Very good figures at any time but when compared with the average contemporary northern town which had up to 70% of it's workforce idle, the figure was quite remarkable. The manager of the Hythe Employment Exchange is on record for having said that he had never had so few names on his books while the chairman of the Dibden Parish Council, was saying that the Hythe tradespeople had "no cause to complain."

The British Power Boat Co. and Supermarine, the largest employers, were about to be joined by the Imperial Airways Flying Boat Base, in providing more jobs than the people of Hythe could entertain. In time for Easter, a new hotel at West Cliff Hall, the former home of Sir Vere Hobart, was to be opened. The Rev. W.H.W. Molyneux, the recent successor at St. John's Church, on being asked about the "wave of prosperity" said that although he hadn't been in the village that long, the villagers were among the most charming he had ever met.

The article continued to discuss the further growth that a recently disclosed expansion of services offered by the ferry proprietors would bring. Despite all the development, it was emphatically stressed, Hythe was losing none of it's charm. It's waterfront and eighteenth century High Street was still very much the centre of the village.

Pier Office, 1930.

Article no. seven was nothing more than a snippet of personal nostalgia. Giving a guided tour of Hythe on January 2, 1937 author Wyndham Hill recalled the days "years ago, when the children were little, a summer time half holiday at Hythe could be very jolly. A tram-ride at the Southampton end, a steamer trip and the plunk-plonk-plunk on the deck of a very long pier were pleasant preliminaries.

Hythe Pier was thronging with sight-seers during the afternoon of April 3, 1936. The occasion, to witness the arrival of the new liner **Queen Mary**, was made worse as Shore Road was flooded and inaccessible because of a high spring tide.

At a meeting of the Dibden Parish Council on May 11, 1936, it was resolved, that a letter be written to the General Estates Co. suggesting that paid yacht's hands should be allowed free landing.

On July 13 they heard of the General Estates Company's opinion that they were being more than generous, already, with the crews of yachts whose owners were members of the Royal Motor Yacht Club whose premises were on the pierhead. The Council persisted that a free landing was urgently needed and urged such a case be put to the Ministry of Transport. That, however, appears to have been the end of the matter.

Earlier in 1936 a twin-screw diesel motor vessel had been ordered from the Essex based Rowhedge Ironworks Co. Ltd. An announcement to this effect appeared in the local press on April 4 when it was also revealed that the new vessel, due for completion in

Hotspur getting assistance at Town Quay mid 1930's.

approximately six months, would eventually operate a half-hourly service with either the **Hampton** or **Hotspur**. The new vessel was launched on the River Colne on November 2 and named **Hotspur II**. Her voyage around the coast to Hythe started two days later but owing to Board of Trade regulations prohibiting her passage at night, she did not arrive until November 7. She was immediately put through proving trials before being accepted on the Hythe passage during the following week. On the commissioning of the **Hotspur II** the **Hampton** was retired and subsequently sold through brokers to shipbreakers in Holland.

The General Estates Company announced at this time that they were holding discussions with the cinema and theatre managements in Southampton and the outcome of which, was hoped, would be a late boat from Southampton to Hythe.

A presentation was made at the Hythe yard on March 15 to Mr. J.G. Finlay, the recently appointed manager of the General Estates Company, to mark the occasion of his wedding. Although he had only been with the company for a few months, Mr. Finlay had made himself very popular with all employees.

On a very cold morning on November 24, 1937 an incident occured that was to be talked about for many months. With the tide receeding fast and snow falling heavily two of the General Estates Company's employees set about preparing the steamer for the first passage across from Hythe to Southampton. It was very dark when shortly before six o'clock Reginald Curtis, slipped from the vessel's slippery deck through the gangway opening and into the water between the head of the pier and the vessel. Curtis cried out as he fell and being a non-swimmer was soon carried away by the fast flowing tide.

Hotspur II being prepared for launching at the Rowhedge Ironworks yard in Essex.

the Southampton Dispensary and Humane Society took place in the Mayor of Southampton's parlour on April 25.

As well as the Mayor, there was also present among others, Reginald Curtis, J.G. Finlay and W.A. Lane (manager and assistant manager of the General Estates Company).

The president of the Southampton Dispensary and Humane Society, opened the proceedings. After reminding those present of the incident he invited the Mayor to make the presentation but not before his own tribute to the hero,

> "without the slightest hesitation, one can say that he saved the life of Curtis. I am sure everyone will agree that was a remarkably brave action and one of which he may be proud."

Despite not being able to see the man in the water, the second employee, who was working below, responded to the cries and leapt in fully clothed. William Charles Longman, found Curtis in a near drowned condition and after a 660 yards struggle taking nearly a quarter of an hour delivered him to safety. The two men made their way to Mr. Longman's home where both were kitted out with dry clothing before returning, somewhat shaken, to their work.

At a meeting of the Dibden Parish Council early in April 1938, it was announced that a full account of the incident had been forwarded to the Royal Humane Society who were about to award their bronze medal and certificate. The presentation along with a gratuity of two guineas from

Launch party for Hotspur II including 3rd right Mr J. G. Finlay, 5th right Mr J. D. Percy and centre Mrs Percy, (widow of Mr T. B. Percy), who performed the ceremony.

Deepdene Cottage, 1935

The Hythe Lido in the late 1930's. This view is now dominated by the Dibden Bay. Reclaimation scheme and proposed site for new Marina.

In his presentation speech the Mayor also paid tribute.

> "Nothing during my year of office can give me greater pleasure than to present you with these tokens. We hear of great bravery on the battlefields and in all sorts of walks of life, but nothing could be more gallant than your act on that November morning. You are the type of Briton whom I am proud to call a friend."

The **Hotspur II** proved very popular with the travelling public as a result from her successful operation on the passage. The original idea for providing this new vessel, was to pave the way for a half-hourly service. A second new vessel was ordered and on delivery the half-hourly service was to be inaugerated. However, while the second new vessel was under construction the volume of traffic expanded by such an extent that the **Hotspur** and **Hotspur II** were unable to cope. Another vessel, the old **Hampton** having been disposed of, had to be found to maintain the faith of the very people for whom the future half-hourly service was designed. The **Carrick Lass**, a wood constructed screw motor vessel, was purchased from a Scottish concern and placed onto the passage during April 1937. The **Hotspur III**, as the new vessel was named, was launched at the end of January 1938. She was almost identical to the **Hotspur II**, being just that fraction larger. Trials were carried out in the River Colne on February 2 and February 3 and she arrived at Hythe over the week-end of February 12 and February 13. She was promptly introduced to the passage with the long promised half-hourly service coming into effect two months later. With traffic expanding almost daily, the sevice showed some encouraging early signs of success. It was to be everything the General Estates Company had hoped of it.

Hotspur III taking the plunge.

On March 2, 1938 a party of Girl Guides (Southampton Dockland) travelled across the passage to Hythe to visit the local company. While walking up the Pier a lighted cigarette was observed thrown from a carriage of the passing train onto the tarred boards of the structure, which were soon burning for about a foot's length. Despite frantic attempts to stamp out the fire, aided by a strong breeze it continued to burn. Meanwhile two of the young fire-fighters had sprinted to the pierhead to fetch a member of the staff, who speedily arrived with a bucket of water.

The Ferry Yard in 1938.

A young passenger on the ferry during the early evening of June 18, 1938 certainly had good reason to remember that particular day. She, was 20 years old Miss Sylvia Bruce of Netley Abbey. The story is best related in her own words.

"As I had the day off on Saturday I decided to go for a swim. I am a keen swimmer but have only been in the water three times this year.

I left my dress and bicycle on the Netley Hard, but half-way across Southampton Water I decided not to turn back as I had intended to do, but to strike out for Hythe. The tide was not coming in very fast when I approached the forest side of the waterway, I found I was treading in soft mud which soon only had a covering of six inches of water.

I am not ashamed to say I got the wind up and shouted as loud as I could for help, because I was knee deep in mud and things weren't getting any better.

Fortunately some very nice people ashore, named, Parsons, heard my cries. They and their friends knew the path through the salty marsh, which was causing me so much trouble and got me out.

I was taken to their home and was lent some clothing. They were exceedingly nice to me and accompanied me across on the Hythe Ferry and saw me on the bus for Netley."

1939 was a very quiet year on the Hythe — Southampton passage until September 3, at 11.00 a.m. British Summer Time to be precise, when war was declared on Germany.

Just a quarter-century after the start of the most frightful conflict in recorded history, Great Britain, and Hythe, was again at war.

Hotspur in Cowes.

War-Time Ferry Part Two September 1939 - May 1945

Locally the "phoney war" didn't appear to upset the pre-war rhythm of everyday life. Come 1940, however, the gravity of the international situation was brought to bare upon the local population. Southampton Water became a restricted area and with that all boat licences were withdrawn. Amateur sailing and fishing (from boats) also prohibited. The "black-out" dimmed the Hythe Pier lights and, indeed, those of the ferries. Just introduced, the half-hourly time-table had to be abandoned for the long established hourly schedule. The **Carrick Lass** was requisitioned by the Admiralty, and subsequently lost. Many of the regular commuters across the passage went off to the war and with them went many of the Hythe Pier and General Estates company's employees.

Among those off to the fight were Commander J.D. Percy, who had succeeded to the head of the companies in 1936, and Mr. J.G. Finlay. The Position of General Manager vacated by Mr. Finlay was offered to and accepted by Mr. W.A. Lane for so long as Mr. Finlay's services were required by the hostilities. As a tribute to all those employees involved, the distinguished war-time career of Commander Percy, Managing Director of both the Hythe Pier and General Estates companies, is briefly outlined hereinafter.

Being a ferry proprietor, he could hardly not have joined the 'grey-funnel line'. Commissioned to **HMS Resolution**, one the Royal Navy's ageing Capital Ships of World War I vintage and some 27,750 displacement tons, he was in 'action' at the Second Battle of Narvik where his ship was struck and had to put into Scapa Flow for repairs. **HMS Resolution** was then deployed to Admiral Somerville's 'Force H' at Malta. Commander Percy's next 'action' was the attack on the occupied French Fleet at Mers-el-Kabir following which **HMS Resolution** was torpedoed while trying to land General de Gaulle and his Free French Army at Dakar.

Commander Percy's next commission was to another Capital Ship, **HMS Queen Elizabeth**, aboard which he sailed from Gibraltar to Alexandria with the last convoy through the Mediterranean. The evacuation of Greece and Crete followed.

Commander Percy was then detailed to Tobruk, where for "outstanding zeal, patience and cheerfulness, and for never failing to set an example of wholehearted devotion to duty" he was honoured with a DSC. The honour came although the garrison fell to constant and accurate enemy shelling during which it was rendered impossible to move Allied troops either in or out of the harbour. Despite the bombardment, Commander Percy escaped aboard a minesweeper but not before he assisted in devising the escape plan. A wreck, the **Liguria**, lying just off shore provided adequate camouflage for thousands of troops to run through her decks and escape via man sized holes, specially cut for the occasion, into waiting evacuation craft.

His Middle East commision lasted until September 1943 when he was appointed

Lt. Commander J. D. Percy in 1945 shortly before his final promotion.

Base Engineer Officer at Leros in the Aegean Sea. The island (Leros) was taken by German paratroopers on November 17, 1943 but the following evening, as darkness descended, Commander Percy escaped with Lord Jellicoe's commandoes aboard an Italian caique, flying a Turkish flag. After a very hazardous journey along the Turkish coast, travelling by night and hiding by day, he eventually reached Cyprus.

He arrived back in Britain in 1944 and married Elisabeth, a Dane whom he had met in London several years previous. After the wedding it was back to sea and to Singapore on VJ Day, not returning home and resuming control of the General Estates and Hythe Pier companies until 1946.

The war-time ferry, continuing its operations, was diverted away from its regular landing steps at the Town Quay between February 21 and February 24, 1940 (inclusive). With the imminent removal of the Floating Dock, temporary moorings, being needed, were laid down on February 21 and 22 closing not only the Hythe Ferry steps but Town Quay shipping berths. The moving of the Floating Dock was effected on February 24.

Early in 1939, the Southampton Harbour Board had authorised and commenced repairs to the landing steps but with the advent of war had them temporarily suspended. This closure presented an opportunity for the repairs, which included providing chequer-treads for and the re-surfacing of the top flight of steps, to be completed in time for the re-opening on February 25.

An incident which could have had tragic consequences but for the presence of mind of one of the Hythe Ferry Staff, occured on June 22, 1941. Two children, Rachel Pusey, aged 13 years, and her 6 years old brother Maurice, were playing in the water close by Hythe Pier on a warm Thursday evening, when Maurice got into difficulties. Rachel attempted to rescue her brother but as she struggled to hold him above the water she too found herself in trouble.

Mr. Charles Randall, the employee, seeing the children, threw off his jacket and plunged from the pier into the water. Both children were subsequently brought ashore, but Maurice, needed artificial respiration and a couple of days in hospital to recover.

The company's property survived all that the enemy had to offer, with the exception of the **Carrick Lass** that is, but the **Hotspur** needed a fortunate escape. Although the exact date appears to have been forgotten, an incident that occured during the course of the war is remembered by many. Under the command of Mr. W. Banks, the **Hotspur**, on passage, triggered off an accoustic mine, it is thought by her disengaged free spinning forward propellor. Both ship and passengers escaped possible disaster with a thorough drenching.

Industry at Hythe, despite the war, was still very active and the source of much of the income of the Hythe-Southampton passage. The Southampton Harbour Board, on February 16, 1943, discussed a letter from the British Power Boat Co. Ltd. at Hythe applying for a site near the Town Quay landing steps for the erection of covered cycle racking for the convenience of their Southampton based employees. It was resolved to allot a site measuring 31ft. 6ins. x 12ft. 0ins. to the east of the Harbour Board's air raid shelters on the Town Quay to be rented to the British power Boat Company.

A similar request from the British Overseas Airways Corporation at Hythe was granted approval on October 19. A site, almost adjacent to that being used by the British Power Boat Company, was decided upon.

Early in August 1943, the General Estates Company were informed by the Southampton Harbour Board of an imminent requisition for the Town Quay by the War Department for a limited, but undetermined, period. Services therefore were diverted to the Royal Pier and became subject to the Harbour Board's statuary tolls. Having always been exempt from such tolls, the patronage of the passage naturally objected. Previous attempts to impose a toll should immediately spring to mind. So High was the feeling that an industrial stoppage was seriously threatened.

At the request of the Military Authorities the tolls were waived, but only on the Southampton Harbour Board's insistance that a claim for the compounded dues would be met by the War Department. The Town Quay restrictions were lifted during mid September.

Lost by the Admiralty in 1940 the Carrick Lass had served on the passage since 1937.

During a meeting of the Southampton Harbour Board Committee on October 8, 1943, it was reported the sum involved amounted to £236 16s. and it was subsequently resolved to press a claim for the amount against the War Department. The claim was not reported as having been accepted and settled until July 14, 1944.

At the same Southampton Harbour Board meeting on July 14 the Clerk also reported the Admiralty requisition of the Hythe Ferry Booking Office on the Town Quay and further the granting of permission to the General Estates Company to place a temporary hut nearby. An acknowledgement rental of 5s per annum was approved.

In 1944, with the long anticipated invasion of Europe imminent, restrictions and censorship were tightened still further. Otherwise, a Royal visit to Hythe shortly prior to D.Day might have been something more of an occasion. The visit being "top secret" was consequently witnessed by very few.

With D.Day approaching Captain James of HMS Squid, the shore based Combined Operations Base at Southampton which was responsible for the administration and housing of a considerable number of the D.Day Assault Squadrons and HMS Squid II, a smaller such base at Hythe, was told of the visit, in utmost secracy, during which His Majesty King George VI would visit the Southampton base and its craft and later procede to Hythe Pier from where a car would receive him and take him to Broadlands, at Romsey.

On the day of the visit a number of sailors detailed for a "special job" were assembled at Hythe Pier. Divided into two parties, one larger than the other, the larger, ordered to adorn their No. 1 dress, were hidden away at the landward end

The train and pierhead have changed little as this 1930's picture shows.

while the smaller, numbering about a dozen and wearing overalls and armed with mops, brushes, brooms and pails, were similarly concealed at the pierhead.

Just before 17.00 the pier train delivered its passengers in time for the 5 o'clock passage to Southampton. As soon as the vessel was away the "working party" emerged from hiding and scrubbed and cleaned the train from end to end in about eight minutes flat before disappearing back into their hide-out. Meanwhile, the "dressed" party had marched down the pier, the column losing a man periodically as the guard ordered for each lampost was taken up.

His Majesty arrived at Hythe Pier, by launch, right on time, just as the last of the 'working party' was hidden away. At the pierhead the King, and his entourage, were received by Commander J.W. Rayner, second-in-command at HMS Squid, who escorted him onto the train and throughout his journey along the pier during which he was saluted by each of the ratings. On arrival at the landward end His Majesty was received by Captain James and after a short pause to talk with the train-driver, Mr. L. Pearce, he and his party proceeded to Broadlands.

A commemorative plaque subsequently placed in the carriage in which the King rode was removed by an anonymous and unscrupulous souvenir hunter.

On May 8, 1945, the German forces surrendered. Despite warnings of there still being uninformed U-Boat captains at sea the lights burned long into the night. Nobody cared. After 2075 days it meant peace again; in Europe at least.

With war over, the Hotspur resumes peacetime employment, pictured here "leaving Hythe down to plimsoll".

Indian Summer 1945 - 1970

Gradually, as restrictions were lifted and soldiers, sailors, airmen, prisoners-of-war, evacuees returned, life began to resume normality.

On May 30, 1945 the General Estates Company arranged for the children of Dibden Purlieu (junior) School an excursion on Southampton Water aboard the **Hotspur**. It, being of an educational as well as recreational nature, met with the full approval of both the Military and Education Authorities. The children were priviledged to see sights that very few persons had been able to see during the previous five years while the waterway had been under restrictions. There were troopships, hospital ships, bailey bridges, floating docks, 'Conondrums' and sections of the world famous 'Mulberry Harbour' to name but a few. The children waved fanatically at each of the ships crowded with G.I.'s and other international troops, giving out a deafening din as their signals were acknowledged. It was the first such trip, too, for skipper J.J. Randall who had as pleasant a time as the children themselves. Similar outings were subsequently arranged for the Hardley (senior) and Hythe (junior) Schools.

At a meeting of the Southampton Harbour Board on September 14, 1945, the lifting of restrictions on amateur boating on Southampton Water and further applications for boatmen's licences was reported. It was resolved to issue licences, but the days of serious competition on the passage were already a part of history.

Late in May 1945 there was a moment of excitement at the Hythe pierhead. An LCP (Landing Craft Personnel) struck the pontoon quite forcibly, causing it to "sway giddily." The LCP was christened "LCP — 'Mary Celeste'" by the contemporary press, for on investigation the craft was found to be unmanned. Apparently it had slipped its moorings at Marchwood, but was not to be a burden on the Hythe Pier Company for long. Only a half-hour after Mr. C. Hosey, a mate on the Hythe Ferry, had gone aboard half expecting "to find at the bottom of the craft, a man lying unconcious, perhaps overcome by engine fumes, or injured," the Military Authorities arrived to claim their property. A few of the pier's piles were damaged as a result of the collision but were subsequently replaced by the Army.

A meeting of the Southampton Harbour Board on May 10, 1946, opened with a report regarding extensive repairs for the Hythe Ferry Landing Steps. It was said that all piling and railing had been renewed in greenheart and that new fender irons had been provided. With the additional replacement of all mooring rings, the berth face was in an almost new condition.

However, despite the work carried out by the Southampton Harbour Board, the General Estates Company wrote to them on June 5, 1946 requesting permission to transfer the landing and embarking of their passengers at Southampton to the new pontoon, at the time under construction at the Town Quay.

Although, at a further meeting of the Harbour Board on July 12, 1946, it was resolved "that further considertion of the matter be deferred and that the Board's officers submit a report on the proposal," nothing was to become of the request.

A copy of a communication, dated January 30, 1947 from the Hythe Pier Company to the Ministry of Transport, received favourable consideration from the Southampton Harbour Board on February 14, 1947. The Hythe concern were seeking approval of their plan to reconstruct the pierhead at Hythe; an operation which would entail extending Hythe Pier by five feet.

The works carried out during 1947 met with a snag towards the end of the year; some old dolphins breaking off just below the mud level on the site of the Pier Pontoon. It was proposed to move the Pontoon 12ft. 3ins. away from the structure in a north-westerly direction and connect by bridge, so that in the event of grounding it would be well clear of the dolphin stumps. The Hythe Pier Company wrote to the Ministry of Transport on January 30, 1948 for permission for this alteration to the original scheme. The letter was discussed on February 13 and once again received their approval.

A little more than a year previous saw the introduction of a new ferryboat, the **Hotspur IV**. She had been built in 1946 at the same yard as the **Hotspur II** and **Hotspur III** by the Rowhedge Ironworks Company. On December 10, Mrs. Elisabeth Percy performed the ceremony which was witnessed by, among others, Commander J.D. Percy, Messrs. T. M. Percy (Director of the General Estates Company) and W.A. Lane (Manager of the General Estates Company). The **Hotspur IV**, flying a 'Union Jack' at her masthead and a 'Red Duster' at her stern, took to the water almost ready for her trials.

Launch of the Hotspur IV December 10, 1946

The **Hotspur IV's** arrival at Hythe marked the end of an era on the passage, however. Although built as a motor vessel, the **Hotspur**, after a subsequent conversion, was the last steamer to ply between Hythe and Southampton. Dispatched to Yarmouth shortly after the **Hotspur IV's** successful introduction to service, the **Hotspur** was to be used for excursions from the town's Britannia Pier taking holiday makers out to Scroby Island, home of seals and wrecks alike, before her eventual disposal and restaurant service.

At 08.00 on December 12, 1946, only two days following the launch of the **Hotspur IV**, the **Hotspur III** set out from Hythe Pier to make a passage to the Town Quay that wasn't to go quite according to plan. It was foggy, but within the limits of safe navigation; until that is, visibility suddenly dropped to no more than a few yards.

A member of the crew, quoting the contemporary press, takes up the story:

"The fog came down when we were half-way between Hythe Pier and the Dock Head. We were proceeding slowly when the **Hampton Ferry** suddenly loomed ahead. The engines were put in reverse and we just touched the other boat. Afterwards we moved round to 49 berth where the passengers disembarked. We remained at 49 berth until the fog lifted and then went to the Town Quay."

Neither the **Hotpsur III** nor the **Hampton Ferry**, a British Railways (Southern Region) train ferry of 2989 gross tons, suffered any damage. Of the 40 persons aboard the Hythe ferry, one female passenger fell and grazed an ankle while the engineer suffered a facial injury. The **Hotspur III** arrived at the Town Quay at 11.45 a.m. and the **Hampton Ferry**, which was moored off Dock Head at the time of the incident, was moved to 37 berth after the fog which limited visibility still further to less than a yard before lifting, cleared.

All the while traffic expanded and the services accordingly. The 1947 Summer time-table, published on March 28, showed from April 1, 34 crossings in each direction daily, except Sundays, and in addition offered excursions on Southampton Water by the **Hotspur IV** each Wednesday. The Winter time-table published as below on October 11 also offered better services than at any time previous.

HYTHE and SOUTHAMPTON FERRY

Half Hourly Winter Service on Weekdays.
Hourly on Sundays From November 1
Southampton Water, Docks, Shipping, Flying Boats, etc., can best be seen from the ferry vessels.

WEEKDAY SERVICE:

Boats leave HYTHE -
6.30 a.m., 6.45 a.m., 7.10 a.m., 7.30 a.m., and every half-hour till 10.30 p.m.
Boats leave SOUTHAMPTON (Town Quay) -
6.52 a.m., 7.0 a.m., 7.30 a.m., and every half-hour till 10.30 p.m., and at 10.45 p.m.

SUNDAY SERVICE:

Boats leave HYTHE -
7.0 a.m., and every hour until 10 p.m.,
Boats leave SOUTHAMPTON (Town Quay) -
7.30 a.m., and every hour until 10.30 p.m.

RETURN FARE:

Adults 1/3, Children (under 12 years), 9d.

SIGHT SEEING WEDNESDAY CRUISES FROM HYTHE PIER WILL BE SUSPENDED AFTER OCTOBER 8 UNTIL NEXT SPRING.

THE GENERAL ESTATES CO. LTD. Tel:Hythe 3203.

At the beginning of October 1947, a local fisherman netting an unexploded bomb, promptly returned it to the water off Hythe Pier. The incident was reported to the Harbour Master, who in turn called in bomb disposal experts. Despite their failure to locate the bomb, the latter were satisfied that it would in no way endanger shipping.

One influence of the war upon the local scene, so far unrecorded, was the deployment of the Empire Flying Boats from Southampton to Durban in 1940. Such a move was necessary as much for

Pierhead showing repositioning of pontoon carried out in 1947.

protection against enemy action as to provide a "vital transport link" between Africa, India and the Middle East. Despite the loss of the Flying Boats to South Africa, Hythe was not to be idle during the war years for it's flying boat maintenance base was actively engaged on urgent repair and general maintenance work for the R.A.F.

The return of the Flying Boats in 1948 was, however, a momentous occasion. The association between the flying Boats and the Port of Southampton began in 1928 when Imperial Airways established a base at Woolston and operated services to the Channel Islands. The base was transferred to Alexandria in 1929 but the proposed inaugeration of the 'Empire Air Mail Scheme' necessitated it's return to Britain, whereby a base was established at Hythe in 1936. It was hardly a base, however; merely a half hanger and hard leased from Supermarine. The runway was a reserved section of Southampton Water below Hythe Pier while the terminal was at 108 berth, Southampton Docks.

After the war, the Flying Boats returned to Britain under the guise of the BOAC's colours, but used a terminal at Poole. A repair and maintenance base was, however, retained at Hythe. The final return to Southampton was effected on March 31, 1948, when the **Harwich**, a Plymouth class vessel, arrived under the command of Capt. A.G. Payne from Iwakuni (Japan) with 21 passengers aboard. The **Harwich** was taxied to a new terminal at Berth 50, arriving, after touching down in a strong gale and tide, at 13.04 hrs.

It is strange how things seem to have a habit of equalling out. First one finds one's spirits up and sooner or later something happens to bring one firmly back to earth. This was very true of Hythe in 1948, albeit in reverse. While spirits were high with the increased employment brought about by the return of the Flying Boats, it was only a matter of months previous when spirits were low due to the winding up of the British Power Boats Company.

Surplus to requirements the Hotspur found herself transferred to the Yarmouth and Gorleston Steamboat Company, extensively modernised and operating from Britannia Pier, Great Yarmouth.

Sadly, the Flying Boat base at Hythe was to survive for less than two years for on March 8, 1950 the BOAC suspended all Flying Boat operations from the Port of Southampton for an indefinite period.

Hythe Pier provided an excellent vantage point for very many curious people on April 27, 1948. A dead basking shark, sighted by an Air Ministry patrol, had been beached in Dibden Bay by Harbour Board staff. As the public ogled, the Harbour Master had the unenviable task of disposing of it.

Basking sharks, which are rare to these waters, can grow up to 40 feet in length. This particular speciman was only 20 feet long and 5 feet in diameter, however, but estimated to weigh some four tons. In the workds of the Air Ministry "It was "stinking to high heaven."

On April 29 the "four tons of rotting flesh" was taken under tow by barge and sunk beyond the Nab.

Fog frequently has hindered the Hythe Ferry time-table and during 1948 this was particularly so. It wasn't all bad in 1948, however. The adverse conditions of late November were followed by an 'Indian Summer' during early December. The Summer season, too, had it's moments. Whit Monday, May 17, was a glorious hot sunny day and queues of people, many with bicycles, formed on the Town Quay for each of the afternoon passages to Hythe. Although rain dampened the festive spirit of the August Bank Holiday Monday the weekend was quite a success on the passage. On Saturday (July 31) and Sunday (August 1) some 2500 and 3000 (respectively) return tickets were sold.

By January 1949 the weather had turned quite inclement. Again fog caused much inconvenience, particularly to the would-be passengers on the last crossing from Southampton to Hythe on January 27. The 10.00 p.m. departure from Hythe took almost three-quarters of an hour to reach the Town Quay and didn't venture out again till very early the following morning, stranding several people overnight. On arrival at Hythe the service was again suspended until the fog eventually cleared at 11.30 a.m.

On February 9 it was high winds causing the inconvenience. Although the "ferry services between Southampton and Hythe were unaffected" the crossings were far from comfortable. A couple of days later, on February 11, despite very thick fog the schedules were maintained, but on February 17, the first passage was not made until 11 o'clock.

By Eastertide the weather had changed dramatically, with the contemporary press reporting April 15 as being "one of the warmest and brightest Good Fridays of the century. All the same, the report went on, "no relief vessels were needed on the Hythe Ferry, where the usual half-hourly service was run."

Indeed, 1949 was to be a Summer to remember.

A proposal for a water-bus service for the people of Southampton, similar to that operating successfully on the Thames, was mooted in the Southern Daily Echo on January 29, 1949. It was suggested that hundreds of persons might use such a service and relieve the already overemployed Hants and Dorset and Southampton Corporation bus and tram services running along the crowded waters edge road between Cobden Bridge, Northam, Bitterne Manor, Woolston, Royal Pier and Redbridge.

A liason with the Hythe Ferry schedule could quite conceivably have proved a boon to both concerns.

An application, in the form of a letter to the Southampton Harbour Board, was made on August 20, 1949 by the Hythe Pier Company for approval of a scheme to place an illuminated advertising sign on the Hythe pierhead. The Master urged a meeting of the Southampton Harbour Board on September 9, not to sanction their approval as in his opinion "from a navigational point of view it would be undesirable to have this kind of illumination within the port area." After some discussion the Hythe Pier Company's motion was rejected.

The Southampton Harbour Board met on April 14, 1950 to discuss a communication dated March 30 from Mr. J.G. Finlay, the General Manager of the General Estates Company, in which the decreasing water depth at the Town Quay landing steps was requested to be restored.

The Harbour Board's Hydrographic Surveyor recommended dredging was requisite and work commenced on June 2.

A Hythe ferryboat crewman saved a situation on March 11, earlier in the year. Some children, playing close by Hythe Pier, found two small brown paper wrapped packages and on opening one, found it to contain some cardboard tubular containers which they took to be fireworks. The crewman, a Mr. Hendy, was shown then and immediately took the packages to a local chemist where it was ascertained that the containers enclosed 300 doses of smallpox vaccine in fine glass capiliary tubes.

Although it was never actually determined just how the packages came to be in the water, it is thought that as the manufactures datemark labelled them unsuitable for use, they were disposed of overboard a passenger liner.

A meeting of the South-West Area Planning Committee at Lyndhurst was reported upon by the Southern Daily Echo on May 19, 1950. The Hythe and District Development Plan had among its many clauses one as follows,

"A larger Pier approach to deal with increased traffic was suggested and it would be necessary to remove the Post Office and a public house on the corner."

The Post Office was resited some years later.

The Hythe Ferry met with a new opposition over the Whitsun Bank Holiday of 1950 which was to develop into its most aggresive rival to this present day. The new opposition was the private motor car. It was not a new opposition in the true sense of the word but since September 23, 1939 had been a very restricted one owing to the limited supplies of motor fuel. However, on May 27, 1950 petrol rationing was officially terminated and thousands of motorists took to the roads as the second-hand car business exploded like it had never been known before.

The Southern Daily Echo reported that "Sotonians seeking a shorter trip by sea to Hythe were not as large as last year." Even so, "seven thousand trippers journied by ferry between Hythe and Southampton during the holiday."

It was a similar tale over the August Bank Holiday but "cyclists and hikers, taking a short cut to the New Forest and the many bathing spots along the coast, kept the Hythe Ferry from Southampton busy."

At a meeting of the Southampton Harbour Board on July 18, 1950, recent negotiations with the General Estates Company regarding their employment of the Town Quay landing steps were discussed. Throughout history this, or to be more specific the financial aspect of it, had been a very vexed question. However in 1950 a very amicable agreement was arranged.

It was estimated that the Harbour Board were spending £150 per annum to maintain the facilities for the Hythe traffic, with a mere £37 being recouped for site

Hotspur IV on Docks Cruise during the early 1950's.

office ground rent and compounded wharfage on goods carried by the ferries, — there being of course an ancient right to a free landing from Hythe. A figure of £300 p.a. was suggested before a communication from the General Estates Company acknowledging the fact that an increased payment was necessary and offering £150 p.a. for two years and £250 p.a. thereafter was read.

After some discussion it was resolved" that the company (General Estates Company) be asked to pay the sum of £200 per annum for the next two years from 1st August, 1950, in lieu of Quay Dues on ships, and tolls on ferry passengers, handled at the Town Quay in connection with the Hythe Ferry, the matter to be reviewed towards the end of that period."

The General Estates Company's reply, dated August 2, accepted these terms.

A ferryboat left Hythe Pier during the evening of September 26, 1950 with an injured man aboard. He had been injured in an accident whilst working nearby Hythe Pier and was taken to the Town Quay from where he was promptly removed to hospital.
The contemporary press reported the incident, on September 27, as having happened "on the Hythe Ferry" but amended their error two days later.

Following the dissolution of the British Power Boats Company in 1948 and the running down of the BOAC Flying Boat Maintenance Base at Hythe throughout 1950, the once busy factory sites along the Hythe shoreline were beginning to take on a sorry look during the Summer of 1950. Although part of the British Power Boats Company's former premises were being occupied by Messrs. BEME Electronic and Marine Equipments Ltd., Victory Transport Ltd. and the Electrical Steam Mining Company (boiler makers and engineers), the properties were grossly under employed.

A ministry of Labour office was established on site to handle the administration of tentative inquiries for factory space and employment. The scheme was rewarded with some early successes as two concerns, Messrs. Scholls (manufactures of foot appliances) and Thermionic Products Ltd. (electronic engineers) took up options. Sadly, however, employment was never to reach the 3000 vacancies offered by the British Power Boats Company, as much to the chagrin of the Hythe Ferry proprietors as to the growing population of the district.

The winter of 1950-51 was comparitively trouble free, there being just one stoppage due to fog on record. On March 1, 1951, the first departures were from Hythe at 11.30 a.m. and from Southampton at 12.00 noon. Both summertime Bank Holidays passed quietly, that of August being spoilt by torrential rain.

View of the High Street during the mid/late 1950's. The large white building is Knighton's, the former Villa Amalthea, now the site of a modern shopping complex.

There was a lot of water about Hythe during 1951, particularly on December 29 when a "phenomenal high tide" flooded much of the village. Access to the ferry was specially uncomfortable as The Marsh and High Street were flooded to a depth of 18 inches. Several men wearing Wellington Boots took the part of Sir Walter Raleigh, but in the manner of the wherrymen of yesteryear Hythe.

The customary fogs returned during the ensueing winter, there being disruptions on October 8, October 15, October 16, 1951, January 30 and March 11, 1952.

By December 1951 the running down of the BOAC Flying Boat Maintenance Base at Hythe was complete even so far as the disposal of the property itself. In a communication to the Southampton Harbour Board on December 7, the Flag Officer Commanding of the Reserve Fleet at Portsmouth gave notice of the Admiralty purchase of the site for use as a base for the commissioning, equipping and laying up of small warships. The Base subsequently became HMS Diligence.

Hythe Pier has seen many great occasions over the years but none more demanding that of July 8, 1952 when an estimated 2,500 persons witnessed the arrival of the s.s. **United States** after her "Blue Riband" earning maiden transatlantic voyage.

"Southern Daily Echo" Shipping Reporter H.A. Taylor in his account of the event on July 9, recorded that "the long pier at Hythe and Weston Shore were absolutely packed."

The pierhead was packed with hundreds of people struggling not just for the best vantage point but for a vantage point at all. All along its 2100 foot length the picture was the same. That estimate of 2500 would seem a conservative one.

Cars were being parked in the approach roads to Hythe and in its surrounding lanes distances of up to a mile from the village centre. Persons, and there were many, not able to get onto the Pier found local residents and hoteliers, some at a price, loaning roof tops and upper windows. Bramshot Hill, Dibden, too, was a well employed vantage point, as was the shoreline each side of Hythe Pier.

The **United States**, the first ocean leviathan built after the war, docked at Southampton at 5.15 p.m. after having captured the celebrated "Blue Riband" from the ever popular **Queen Mary**.

"Thousands of people ashore or afloat in the biggest assembly of craft to use Southampton Water since D.Day 1944" wrote H.A. Taylor, "yesterday gave the new Blue Riband holder **United States** the biggest welcome ever accorded a liner in the history of the port." Unbeknown to the multitude and the reporter alike was the fact that they were witnessing almost the last such occasion.

Captain Henry Thomas Banks pictured aboard the Hotspur August 1935.

September 28, 1952 was a sad day for those associated with the Hythe Ferry. At the age of 85 and with more than 60 years of employment on the passage behind him, Henry Thomas Banks died after a short illness at his home in Prospect Place, Hythe.

Henry Thomas Banks, or as he was more affectionately known — Harry Banks, began his career as a deckboy on the old paddlers **Frederica** and **Hotspur**, working his way to skipper in brisk time. On June 23, 1909 he earnt a local pilot's certificate following a searching examination. He was also a very successful yachtsman in his time and won many prizes in local regattas. Upon reaching retirement age he refused his pension firmly believing that should he stop working then his life would end too, something bourne out in time for his death fell within three months of his long postponed retirement. He did surrender his command of the ferry boats some 17 years previous, however, and was thereafter employed on Hythe Pier splicing and repairing ropes and in various other shore duties.

Mr. Henry Thomas Banks left a widow and two sons, both employed on the passage. Mr. John Banks was the piermaster at Hythe and Mr. Harry Banks, another former skipper, being a member of the shore staff, also at Hythe.

The Southampton Harbour Board's financial arrangement with the General Estates Company due to expire on July 31 had been discussed with the Hythe Ferry proprietors and a settlement agreed upon, before the Board met on July 14, 1953. For a period of five years from August 1, 1953 the General Estates Company had agreed to pay the Southampton Harbour Board the sum of £250 per annum in lieu of Quay Dues on ships, and tolls on ferry passengers, handled at the Town Quay in connection with the Hythe Ferry and in addition from January 1, 1954 they should pay the statutory toll of 3d for each passenger brought by coach for embarkation on the ferry for sightseeing trips. A return of these passengers to be submitted to the Southampton Harbour Board on a monthly basis.

On December 13, 1953 the Greek 17,434 gross tons passenger liner **Olympia** which had only been commissioned two months previous ran aground close by Hythe Pier and the old BOAC jetty, then part of HMS Diligence. The ship was promptly pulled clear by three tugs and towed out into the main shipping channel.

There have been fishing competitions staged from Hythe Pier almost since it's construction in 1880. One staged by the Southampton Sea Angling Club on July 18, 1954 was memorable for a couple of reasons. It was the second in their summer series from the structure but like the first did not yield a big catch. In fact only 40 fish weighing 21 lbs. 0¼ ozs. were shared between the 56 participants. What made it a memorable contest was the two unusual fish landed. The overall winner of the heat, Mr. W. Ellerington, caught a 12 ozs. grey mullet and Mr. H. Churcher landed a 9 ozs. mackerel. Grey mullet had been caught before, albeit very occasionally, but nobody could remember a mackerel.

The winter of 1954-1955 produced a right mixture of nasties. On November 18 fog reduced visibility to a mere ten yards and the first ferry from Hythe was therefore delayed till 11.30 a.m. Fog affected services the following day too when all ferries after 6.00 p.m. were cancelled.

During the morning of December 8 a violent gale swept across Southampton Water. So treacherous were conditions that the ferry ceased to operate at 9.00 a.m. when the high tide reached deck level on Hythe Pier. Buildings at the shore and of the pier were flooded by "the highest tide seen for many years." Both Shore Road and West Street were impassable while Prospect Place, High Street and parts of Jones Lane were flooded. There was more than a foot of water in The Marsh.

The violent sea knocked down the low wall at the rear of the Lord Nelson public house, flooding the beer garden and floating it's tables and chairs. A part of the International Stores in the High Street was also demolished as the seas advanced into the warehouse.

The gales continued throughout the day but the floods retreated with the ebbing tide. However the next tide during the evening produced another flood.

Further fogs were experienced on December 11, when the first departure from Hythe did not leave until 8.30 a.m. and on December 18, when after the first boat to Southampton got away on time at 6.30 a.m. the fog thickened so much that the schedule had to be abandoned until 10.00 a.m. There was snow too, albeit light, on January 4. A lot of care had to be taken by passengers and crew alike on the slippery decks of the boats and the pier but the thaw came during the night of January 5 without a mishap on record.

Whit Monday, May 30, 1955 was Day 3 of a national rail strike and many Sotonians were compelled to find their amusement locally. It was a fine day and thousands took to the water, many travelling across the passage to Hythe although not in the numbers of by-gone days.

One of the Hythe Ferry's rivals came in for some harsh critisism in a letter published in the Southern Daily Echo's "Echo" Letter-box column on July 9, 1955, while in the same communication the ferry service received a morale boosting pat on the back.

Drummond Arms from High Street, mid 1950's.

The Marsh circa 1955.

Fawley Bus Service.

This week the general public has been confronted with the news that the Hants and Dorset Motor Services Ltd. are advancing fares on various routes, and I understand that the increase in some cases will be as much as 7d on a present 2s 5d return.

Since the end of the war instead of the service on the Fawley route improving there has been the reverse. The bus company claim they are short of vehicles and are not able to improve this service, but let us hope with the extra monies from fare increases they will be able to purchase new rolling stock thereby to improve matters for the public benefit.

Perhaps the time is now ripe for the Hythe Ferry Co. Ltd. to put on three boats an hour. If they can do this I am sure the people on this side of the water will be grateful. One must give them full marks for the good time keeping of their services to the public.

Whilst winding up his day's duties on July 14, 1955 General Estates Company employee Leonard Cavill found his services requisite of the local constabulary.

Mr. Cavill whose usual employment during the 12 months he had been working for the General Estates Company was engineer on the ferry boats, was on that particular day operating the Hythe Pier railway.

Among the passengers using the train which had met the last boat, the 10.45 p.m. from Southampton, were five civilian clothed sailors from HMS Diligence. As the five men were leaving the pier a Police Constable on duty at the Pier entrance apprehended them and questioned one about a pint glass he had in his hand. Not being satisfied with the explanation the constable invited the sailor, who offered no resistance, along to the Police Station (New Road). They hadn't gone a few yards when one of the other four delivered from behind a hefty blow to the Constable's jaw. The constable immediately sank to his knees but managed to hold his attacker by the legs and pull him to the ground.

Mr. Cavill who witnessed the assault from the pier office immediately ran to render assistance and together he and the constable completed an arrest.

At the Police Station the assailant was charged with assault. His colleague, who admitted stealing the pint glass from a Southampton public house, was referred to the Southampton Police who subsequently dealt with the matter. The Constable's injuries amounted to a swelling on the left side of his jaw and a pain in the back, but he remained on duty.

A sailor appeared before the Hythe Magistrates Court on July 22 where he was fined £5 on a plead of "guilty". The local constabulary said that "had it not been for the assistance by Mr. Cavill, there is no doubt this attack would have developed into a much more serious offence."

The presiding magistrate, too, spoke for Mr. Cavill. "I should like to express appreciation of Mr. Cavill's action in supporting the police. He should be congratulated for his gallant assistance."

For many years some discomfort had been caused due to a lack of toilet facilities at the Hythe Pier entrance. The Hythe Pier Company have always provided their patronage with such facilities but only at the pierhead. As many ferry passengers transferred to and from buses at the entrance to the pier it was generally felt that something was needed in the immediate locality — Hythe's public conveniences being in Shore Road opposite the factory sites and closeby the railway station, a distance of at least a half-mile.

It was intended to incorporate the building of public conveniences at the desired place when the modifications to the Hythe Pier approach suggested in the Hythe Development Plan were effected, but there were problems. It had been moved by the New Forest Rural District Council to find a site in the vicinity of the Hythe Pier entrance and neighbouring bus depot and arrange for it's purchase. A site subsequently became available but a price could not be agreed and so at a meeting of the New Forest Rural District Council early in November 1955 the question of a compulsorary purchase of the site was considered.

Opinion was expressed in the chambers that the conveniences should be established in the New Road car park, but

Dibden Post Office, late 1950's.

there was a problem over local opposition. There was strong opposition in the chambers, too, as 160 buses a day stopped in the Hythe Pier approach and that during the Summer months there were additional buses and coaches. The Hythe Ferry was moving 600 persons an hour so how it was asked could a decision to build the facilities in question in the car park, 300 yards away, be justified. It was urged that a "site at the pier and not the car park should be of paramount importance to the Council" and a view was added that should the conveniences be built in the car park there would still be complaints about the lack of such facilities at the Hythe Pier entrance.

The New Forest Rural District Council decided to go ahead with a compulsorary purchase order for the site at the Hythe Pier entrance.

Westcliffe Hall Hotel, once the home of Sir Vere Hobart and one of the very few of Hythe's former large houses still surviving.

A Ministry of Housing and Local Government inquiry was held at the Lyndhurst Public Offices during December 1955 following a decision by the New Forest Rural District Council to refuse a development plan for 30 two-bedroom bungalows on a seven acre site just off the main road at Dibden.

It appears there was a popular belief thriving, among the local community that Hythe was to be developed as a dormitory town for Southampton.

Although Hythe still retained much of it's old-world charm even so far as to allow forest ponies to roam freely right into it's very heart, the population was growing at an astronomical rate, and it needed housing. A large new council owned estate was by this time in an advanced state of build on what was once Sir Robert Hobart's Langdown Estate. When the first of the new houses was occupied on March 3, 1952 all that remained of the old estate, apart from it's deteriorating centrepiece — Langdown House, was the name of both property and owner perpetuated for posterity. The new complex became known as Langdown Estate and Sir Robert's name was given to one of it's streets — Hobart Drive. Other streets carry some famous names too.

Another housing complex commissioned by the New Forest Rural District Council during the 1950's was that, later to be known as the Netley View Estate, at Buttsash announced in the contemporary press on November 11, 1958 and commenced the following year.

A large private development was taking place, while the dormitory fears prevailed, on the old golf course. The street names for this new Hollybank Estate, which was later extended to include Lanehays Copse, were derived from a competition held among local schoolchildren. Another private development of the fifties was undertaken by the Esso Petroleum Company, for the tennancy of their employees, on land acquired between the Langdown Estate and the extremes of their own land so far as Frost Lane.

To cater for the expanding population and to relieve the overburdened shops of the High Street, a new parade of shops was opened, some in time for Christmas, during December 1958 on the site of Pylewell House, once a landmark of the old village. Frontages of the 20 new shops were in both The Marsh and Pylewell Road while storing access was from School Road. Small parades were also built on each of the housing estates.

From a purely selfish point of view the General Estates Company could only have benefited from the dormitory idea.

While the General Estates Company revelled in much of that taking place during the late fifties they must have been a little apprehensive about a part of the insurance against the dormitory idea. A new road linking Calshot to the Totton

By-pass was approved by both district and county councils and started during the latter years of the decade. The first section of the road, which was designed to speed commercial traffic from the existing industries at Fawley and Hythe along it's way and be adaptable in catering for those it was hoped it would attract, known as the Marchwood By-pass, was opened on July 11, 1960 after two years of construction at a cost of £375,000. Stage two of the scheme, the Hythe By-pass, had been approved during 1959 with a tender of £260,500 being accepted by the Hampshire County Council on November 23. The road was completed by the mid-sixties.

Hythe Pier was visited on February 6, 1957 by Sussex police making inquiries into the disappearance of a prominent man after his yacht had been found washed ashore at West Wittering the previous day. From the enquiries at Hythe, the Sussex police ascertained that the mising man's yacht, the **Dunessa**, a 15 ton motor cabin cruiser which he had hired under an assumed name on December 12, 1956, had anchored off the pier on February 4. During the morning the man had rowed to the pier in a ten foot dinghy, moored it alongside and asked the piermaster "to keep an eye on it". No particular attention was shown as such requests were commonplace. He collected his dinghy at about lunchtime and rowed back to his yacht, sailing away shortly afterwards. It would appear he had crossed to Southampton on the ferry as a return ticket issued on February 4 was among belongings found in the yacht.

Hythe Pier had a narrow escape from collision during the afternoon of July 9, 1958. A Panamanian passenger liner, the 8,929 gross ton **Arosa Kulm**, ran aground stern first desperately close to the pierhead. The rising tide allowed seven tugs to free her, but only after a ninety minute struggle.

At a meeting of the Southampton Harbour Board on September 16, 1958, it was reported that the agreement by which the General Estates Company paid to the Southampton Harbour Board the compounded sum of £250 per annum in lieu of Quay Dues on their vessels and Tolls on passengers carried in connection with the Hythe Ferry and in addition the statutory toll of 3d for each person embarked from coaches for sightseeing trips, had expired on July 31.
A recommendation that the Southampton Harbour Board fix a new figure of £260 per annum for the compounded dues and that the agreement be for a further five years on July 31, 1963 was approved. Since this time, the compounded dues have been reviewed annually, generally rising along the lines of inflation.

The following correspondence had appeared in the Southern Daily Echo's feature "Echo Letter-box" on September 9, 1958.

> "There have, in the past, been many suggestions as to what can be done about the traffic jams which occur regularly on the Totton Causeway, particularly at the peak period.
> As these jams are caused mainly by workers from Fawley, Marchwood, surely the answer would be to run a floating bridge or ferry service across Southampton Water for these workers landing at the Royal Pier?"

Where could "Car Driver" of Woodlands near Southampton have been for the previous **** years.

Although the Flying boat Base at Hythe had closed with the departure of the BOAC in 1950, Flying Boats were still operating from the Berth 50 Terminal in Southampton Docks and were often viewed by ferry passengers whilst on passage or from Hythe Pier.

However, Aquila Airways who had been operating various types of Flying Boats on an assortment of services out of Southampton for almost a decade flew their final flight using a Solent Class Flying Boat, the **Awatere** to Madeira on September 26, 1958.

Southampton, which had been the first British port to have a marine air base back in 1919, retained it's licence to operate a water aerodrome, although it was never to be used again.

The Waterside Art Group held it's third exhibition of works on Hythe Pier between May 14 and May 19, 1959. There were 92 finished pictures and 19 "exercises" by 26 artists on display. Admission was free of charge between 2.00 and 8.00 p.m.

A new decade opened with some heart-warming news for the district. On January 7, 1960 the Admiralty announced that a contract for civillian management of HMS Diligence had been awarded to White's Shipyard (Southampton) Ltd. effective from April 1, 1960, offering employment for 100 men. Admiralty status after March 31 was for only five or six to act as "agents for the operational authority of the ships." HMS Diligence, which was first commissioned on March 3, 1953 and manned when at it's peak by 35 officers and 500 men, was to retain its reserve fleet function.

The future of it's officer's mess was, however, uncertain. The mess, vacated on March 31 also, was the crumbling mansion of Langdown House. This building, once the magnificent heart of Sir Robert Hobart's country estate, had been gradually deteriorating since Sir Vere Hobart's move to the Isle of Wight during the 1930's when it passed into the hands

Once the home of Sir Robert Hobart and more recently HMS Diligence, Langdown House was demolished in 1963.

of Mr. S.S. Taylor. It had been built as long ago as 1797 and was first owned by Mr. George Tate, whose name is another of those perpetuated among the streets of the Langdown housing estate. The Hobart family took possession in 1849. During World War II it became a hostel and afterwards it's association with HMS Diligence was born when the BOAC acquired the property for use as a store. On the Admiralty occupation in 1953 it regained a little of its pride as the officers of HMS Diligence moved in. The pride was short lived, however, as during mid-November, 1961, it was sold for demolition under auction. The successful bid was £30,000, after bidding had started at £15,000. Despite last minute efforts by the Dibden Parish Council to have the property preserved for it's architectural value it was bulldozed flat in March 1963 to make way for a private housing development.

But for the name of the housing complex and one of it's streets, the Hobart's Langdown Estate had gone forever.

Police activity was rife around Hythe Pier at the end of June 1960, when they were looking for a man in his early twenties who had accosted a nine years old girl as she rode her pony across the heath near Dibden Purlieu, attempted a sexual assault and strapped a tie, tightly around her neck. The attack took place on June 27 at a place where the girl frequently exercised her pony. The police search centred around Hythe Pier because as recorded by the Southern Daily Echo on June 29, "the wanted man is believed to have travelled to Hythe from Southampton at about lunchtime on Monday (27th)". The newspaper added the following plea: "Any persons who travelled on the Hythe ferry, or on buses into or out of Hythe on Monday and saw a passenger answering the attacker's description are also asked to call at Hythe police station." Not yielding as much information as desired from it's Hythe Pier centre, the search was considerably stepped up at the location of the incident where police were stopping every vehicle and questioning every person crossing the Beaulieu Heath. Then, on July 1, it was dramatically switched back to Hythe Pier, as it came to the light that a man answering the attacker's description had boarded a Lymington — Hythe Ferry bus on the heath close to Dibden Purlieu, getting off at the ferry, on the day in question. The bus connected with the 5.30 p.m. ferry to Southampton and so it was assumed the man travelled across the passage. All persons who had travelled on the bus and/or ferry were urged to search their memories and report to the police, a major clue being a box camera in a canvas case with shoulder strap thought to have been carried by the attacker. The bus conductor, had told police that the man was picked up at an isolated "stop" and that he bought a single ticket to and disembarked at the Hythe Ferry, travelling quite relaxed on the upper deck. A 19 years old man was charged with "intent to murder" at Lymington on July 5.

A major dispute between the operators of the local bus routes, and several local groups and companies, including the General Estates Company, erupted in 1960. It arose from the bus company's introduction of a new timetable. The Dibden Parish Council discussed and rebuked the new timetable at a meeting on March 3. Under the old timetable every bus, except the occasional works special, stopped at the Hythe Ferry but under the new one almost half of them by-passed Hythe altogether along Southampton Road. It was agreed to send the following telegram to the company,

"Urgent. Essential reinstate old services

immediately to avoid complete chaos in Hythe. Our views are being sent by letter to Minister of Transport."

The meeting was of the opinion that the new timetable was designed so that there would be "no tie-up with the ferry times." This was the real bone for contention so far as the General Estates Company were concerned, for many bus passengers from Buttsash, Holbury, Blackfield, Langly, Lepe, Exbury, Fawley and Calshot prefered to break their journey to Southampton at Hythe and continue by ferry. Perhaps more than a just a thought behind the design of the new bus timetable.

A meeting, called by the Dibden Parish Council, was held on March 15 and attended by representatives of the Council, Fawley Parish Council, General Estates Company, several factories and other businesses of the Hythe area and the Hants and Dorset Motor Services Ltd. The bus company did acknowledge that certain difficulties had arisen from their new timetable and told that remedial measures had been made on March 14. Regarding connections with the ferry a Hants and Dorset Motor Services Ltd. representative told how his company's new timetable made provisions for two buses an hour in each direction to meet the Hythe — Southampton Ferry and that all drivers were instructed to await the arrival of the ferry-boat. The two parish council's were still not satisfied and negotiations continued. At a meeting of the Dibden Parish Council on May 2 it was reported that an agreement had been made with the bus company to route further buses through Hythe as from June 5. So far as the General Estates Company were concerned connections were in accordance with their half-hourly schedule.

For some unknown reason, the most important event of 1960 seems to have taken place almost unnoticed and cetainly without the pomp and ceremony usually accorded such an occasion. Very early in the year the General Estates and Hythe Pier companies moved their operations from their Hollybank House headquarters to Hotspur House, a new and spacious building off Prospect Place. The building created a lot of interest as it took shape and a certain amount of horror as it neared completion. An opinion shared among many local residents was that it did not comply in any way with the surrounding conservation area.

The successful tender was that of Messrs. Brazier & Son Ltd. of Southampton, who, on November 8, 1958 had quoted the sum of £12,611 for the work, which began on January 21, 1959. A privilege afforded the building workers for the duration of the construction was a concessionary pass to free transportation across the passage, something which created a certain bond between the men and the General Estates Company resulting in the building being completed in little more than eight months despite several delays resulting from a number of amendments.

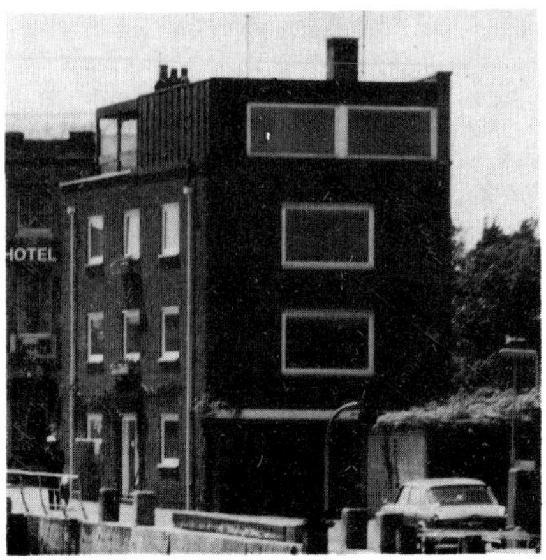

Hotspur House opened in 1960 with subsequent penthouse extension. (Alan Titheridge)

Messrs. Rawlence and Squarey, of Southampton, were the architects behind the project which included many of Mrs. Elisabeth Percy's original ideas in it's design. The rectangular three story building is equipped with an integral garage and offices on the ground floor, offices on the first and a flat "above the shop" on the second. A "penthouse" extension to the flat has been subsequently added by the same contractor who was also engaged to carry out some extensive alterations. Commander J.D. and Mrs. Percy moved into the flat, which commands some excellent views of the pier, passage and Southampton Water in general, during the early days of November 1959 being followed very early in 1960 by the General Estates and Hythe Pier companies. Towards the end of the contract Messrs. Brazier & Son Ltd. were further engaged to assist with design work for the Hythe Pier entrance. This work was subsequently carried out by Messrs. P. Trant Ltd. who provided sliding gates and modifications to the Ticket Office.

Some bizarre and colourful people in the guise of contemporary "beatniks" and "teddy-boys" were conveyed across the passage over the 1960 August Bank Holiday week-end. They were all en route to Lord Montagu's Fifth Beaulieu Jazz Festival, staged in the grounds of Palace House on August 1. Regretably the occasion was marred by a "riot". Lord Montagu had much opposition to his festivals and made few friends from the "Beaulieu Battle." Regular passengers on the Hythe — Southampton ferry who shared the crossing with the festival-goers suffered no inconvenience, however, except perhaps from out-of-tune guitars and untrained voices.

The withdrawal of Flying Boat operations almost a decade previous was a loss for the sightseers on Hythe Pier but the setting up of an establishment to research further into the contemporary invention of the hovercraft close by on October 1, 1960 provided an alternative for the curious. Under the charge of Mr. C.S. Cockerell, the inventor of the hovercraft, the research establishment offered employment for some thirty engineers on a site at St. John's Park, formerly part of HMS Diligence purchased from the Admiralty under the civilianisation programme. Offices were subsequently constructed in The Grove, a large and attractive house on site. Hovercraft of all sizes, including the celebrated SRN 1, were soon commonplace off the Hythe waterfront and pier.

1961, palindromic in print as was it's course. The ferry, had enjoyed a trouble and incident free period during January and February, but on March 9, 1961, after having set out on the 9.00 a.m. crossing from Hythe Pier only a minute or two previous, the **Hotspur II** came into collision with a barge being pushed by a tug. Damage to either vessel was slight and both were able to continue with the minimum of delay. The **Hotspur II** delivered her 30 passengers to the Town Quay only a few minutes late, some apparently unaware anything had even happened, and made the return journey, on time, at 9.30 a.m. One day later, a Bomb Disposal Unit from HMS Vernon was called to attend an unexploded mortar bomb just off Hythe Pier. The device which had been discovered lodged behind a boulder was safely removed at low tide.

Both Hythe Pier and the ferry boats proved excellent vantage points for sightseers on April 25, 1961. The Cunard liner **Ivernia** with 455 Canada bound passengers on board had run aground in heavy rain and a strong wind just 300 yards slightly to the north of the Pier. Unfortunately for the liner the grounding occured on an ebbing tide. Despite the attempts of nine tugs to free her she had to wait until the evening's high tide, all the while the Hythe ferries having to make wide detours to avoid the wash from the tugs which were pulling against a wind constantly threatening further grounding. Further difficulties were experienced by the ferry boat captains as they came alongside the pier pontoon, it bobbing about like a bouy in the heavy swell. Upon a successful refloating late in the day, the **Ivernia** was returned to berth where divers inspected her bottom before she eventually got under way, on April 26.

Towards the end of May and during the first week of June, 1961 a film crew making a half-hour colour industrial film on behalf of the Hythe electric blanket manufactures Messrs. Easipower Appliances Ltd. shot several sequences on the Hythe ferries and Pier. The film, to promote a new award winning electric blanket, was intended for business gatherings and symposiums nationwide. Under the title of "Visit to Dreamland", the film showed a visitor being taken from the company's Southampton head-office across the passage, the way of many a factory worker, to the Hythe factory in Shore Road. He was then given a tour of the factory to witness the manufacture of the "Dreamland" blanket. Some fine photography went into the production, including some magnificent panoramic views from the roof of Southampton's mighty South-Western Hotel taking in the width of the city and Southampton Water across to Hythe.

Fishing off Hythe Pier had for a considerable time been something of a joke. On September 10, 1961 the joke became a little less funny for the 34 members of the Southampton Sea Angling Club in competition from the structure. Ten members caught a mere thirteen fish, weighing 7 lbs 4¾ ozs., between them, "the second worst result since the war". Many reasons for the decline in the number of fish have been put forward over the years, modern technology probably having much to do with it.

February, 1962 saw the retirement, after 41 years service with the Hythe — Southampton Ferry, of Mr. Thomas Longman, aged 78 years. "Tommy" Longman had been the train driver for many years until 1946 when he took over in the Hythe Pier Ticket Office.

The workaday routine of the Hythe passage was suddenly thrown into confusion during the evening of September 13, 1962, with a derailment of the Hythe Pier train. Mr. Thomas Phillips, the train driver, told the contemporary press, "I was actually braking to come into the platform to stop and the tractor jumped into the air, shot across the lines and steeplechased over the sleepers. I had a few bruises and the drivers seat is a hard one and is not meant for steeplechasing. As a result of the accident, the live rail was short-circuited and all the lights went out in the train. There was no panic among the passengers and I think they were more amazed than anything else when the train suddenly stopped and all the lights went out. People came dashing out from outside the pier to see what had happened". The train was just returning to the pier entrance station with a complement of 20 passengers off the 9.00 p.m. ferry from the Town Quay when the accident happened. A fitter, Mr. J.C. Nixon, was immediately summoned from his home and soon had the engine back on the lines. However, the emergency recovery operation was to no avail as the trains electrical pick-up gear was damaged in such a way that the train could not be re-commisioned that night. Mr. Nixon also discovered something of a more serious nature upon investigation of the scene of the crash — a wooden wedge which had undoutedly been the cause of the derailment. It was a simple deduction that the wedge had assumed it's poisonous position very shortly before the incident, as the train had left the pier entrance station not ten minutes previous to meet the nine o'clock ferry from the Town Quay, crossing the very spot on the way. How it came to be there was a mystery, however. Although nobody present was able to report seeing anything suspicious it was concluded that it had been placed there deliberately, the police being informed accordingly. One theory worked upon by the local constabulary was that a sabateur could have arrived on the scene completely unobserved by means of one of the steel ladders from the pier decking to the shore behind the shops in the High Street from where access and escape could have been effected via the public throughfare at the Post Office or the beer garden of the Lord Nelson public house. The case has never been solved.

October 1962 saw happier times for the Hythe Pier Railway. It caught the eye of the local press on October 3, being one of the few private railways operating on the first day of a national rail strike. On October 29 the train made an extra-special journey along the pier, gaily decorated with white ribbons and sporting a large white placard enscribed "Hythe Honeymoon Express". The occasion was the wedding, the daughter of Mr. E. Carter, the proprietor of the pierhead restaurant. The train was employed to taxi the happy couple and their guests along Hythe Pier to a reception in the restaurant following the wedding ceremony which had taken place at St. John's Church earlier.

The winter of 1962/63 with fogs, sleet, snow, blizzards and storms was to be the most severe in recent history.

On October 17 the "worst fog of Autumn" prevented all departures before eleven o'clock. A two and a half hour delayed start and a half hour break disrupted the morning of October 18. On December 4 all mid morning services had to be cancelled.

Snow fell on November 16 but only slight causing no problems for the Hythe passage with regard to slippery decks on both ferries and pier. The snow that fell on December 27 was, however of a very different nature. It fell so thick that at times during the day the Hotspur skippers could hardly see the bows of their vessels. By the morning of December 28 almost eight inches of snow covered the neighbourhood.

1963 arrived with no let-up in the arctic conditions. Indeed, it wasn't until January 26 that a thaw started and that was short lived as by January 30 frost had returned to be followed by further snow on February 2. A "great thaw" was promised by the "weather men" on February 7 with blue skies, bright sunshine and temperatures in the forties being the order of February 8. It snowed again, quite heavily, on February 11 but quickly thawed leaving slush about for days afterwards.

October 3, 1962 the first day of a national rail strike but the Hythe Pier train continues unabated.

"Is this the hardest winter you remember"? some of the residents of Racketts, a home for the elderly and once one of Hythe's large private houses, were asked by a local newspaper correspondent. "No", being the unanimous response. Mr. Jesse Waterman, a 78 years old former High Street green-grocer, told of a winter towards the end of the nineteenth century when Southampton Water froze over for two weeks and it was possible to walk from Hythe Pier to the Southampton Dock Head. He further remembered "icebergs" and the fear of both damage to both pier and boats.

The winter referred to was probably 1894/95 when although Southampton Water never actually froze, icefloes, rather than icebergs, some a couple of acres in extent, were a constant menace to the ferries and shipping in general. One would have had to have been very brave to make the walk across but without a wind it was possible. Many years previous, however, it was definitely possible to walk from Hythe to Southampton. On January 23, 1830, before the **Emerald** had introduced steam communications to the passage, the Hampshire Advertiser recorded,

"We have this week seen our river frozen so far down as to suspend the water communications between this town (Southampton) and Hythe, a width of about two miles".

An amusing incident dates from this time. Early in February 1963 a man walked into a shop in the Hythe High Street and asked where he could get the next bus to Cowes. Upon a startled look from a bemused shop assistant he asked, "This is Ryde isn't it"?

A similar misunderstanding occured during August 1963. This time a gentleman not only arrived at Hythe mistaking it for Cowes but booked into the Drummond Arms Hotel. It wasn't until the following morning when at breakfast he asked the way to Saunders Roe (Cowes) he learnt of his error.

"They told me to get this boat for the island", he explained.

Many hundreds of enthusiastic and excited people crossed the passage during the evening of April 3, 1963. All were bound for the Dell, the home of Southampton Football Club who were hosts to Nottingham Forest Football Club in an F.A. Cup Sixth Round Replay.

Each boat from late afternoon until seven o'clock was packed with expectant supporters of the rank outsiders from the depths of the Second Division who had travelled north and drawn with First Division opposition just a few days previous. Thousands of supporters were locked out when the gates were closed long before kick-off with many having to make an early return to Hythe.

Those who followed after 9.30 p.m., however, were in jubilant mood. For they had seen the "Saints" cancel out a 0-3 half-time deficit and almost win in extra time. Stories have it that the roar for the equaliser was heard by the Hythe Ferry crewmen. History reveals that Southampton won a second replay only to falter against the legendary Manchester United at the penultimate hurdle.

When Mr. James Percy had the first **Hotspur** built in 1889, his vessel arrived from Plymouth with a black hull and black funnel. A white band was subsequently added to the funnel to complete the livery perpetuated in each subsequent vessel including Commander J.D. Percy's **Hotspur II**, **Hotspur III** and **Hotspur IV**. However, on April 5, 1963 Mr. J.G. Finlay, the manager of the General Estates Company, announced a policy decision to experiment with a blue and cream colour scheme on one of the "Hotspurs".

"If the colour stands up to the rough treatment", added Mr. Finlay, "we may repaint the other boats".

Towards the end of June, the **Hotspur IV** emerged from her annual dry inspection with a medium blue hull and cream funnel with white band. It was an immediate success with the patronage of the passage, the new colours creating an airy and summery effect The colour quality was obviously a success too, as the **Hotspur II** and **Hotspur III** subsequently acquired new livery, using slightly darker blues.

As the sixties progressed several slight modifications to paintwork were carried out resulting in a situation whereby no "Hotspurs" were exactly alike.

For the residue of 1963 and the main part of 1964 there was a famine of news. A similar situation had existed "seventy years ago", so "somebody had the bright idea of sending a reporter to Hythe for the day". The Hampshire Advertiser reporter's account was published in a letter to the newspaper under the pseudonym "Rambler", much, (as follows), being reprinted in the Southern Evening Echo on February 28, 1964.

> "Attracted by an advertisement in your columns of cheap trips to Hythe I one day last week took advantage of a fine day and made a journey to that picturesque little village. Asking a constable at the Town Quay where the Hythe steamer started from, that good-natured officer politely pointed to a peculiar shaped vessel lying off the Town Quay steps.

This ship was named the **Hampton** and was commanded by a bluff old salt, who was evidently proud of his own voice, for he was to be heard far and near giving most peremptory orders as to the loading of his vessel.

After a journey of about 12 minutes during which the engines were well handled by "Black Sam", a real good old chappie, we arrived at Hythe Pier, but instead of stopping we proceeded on our way to Netley and this surprised me greatly. I shouted out to the skipper that we had passed Hythe.

He was much annoyed at my interference and bawled out that he was commander and knew his business. A few minutes afterwards he shouted down the speaking tube "Stoppie" and ultimately the vessel "stoppied" and returned to the pier head ....

On leaving the pier my ticket was demanded by an eagle-eyed official at the gate, who seemed to combine business with pleasure for I noticed he was actively engaged separating two fighting cocks ....

In order to gain some knowledge of the inhabitants I approached an old man, "a native" .... He bemoaned the decline in the prosperity of the village, attributing it to the absence of the rich people who formerly possessed estates there.

The "good old gentry" had died out and half-bred snobs had succeeded them who had new fangled ideas about street-lighting, drainage and a thousand other so-called improvements, all very well in their way, but not to be obtained without a heavy increase in the rates which the poor cottagers are unable to bear ....

I could not admire this old man's standstill opinions but he delighted me with a description of the village and the people in it, from which I gathered it to be a rather clannish place, there being many people of the same name or family.

My time being up I thanked him and on running to catch my boat I had to pass through a crowd of people at the pier gates who were concerned in watching intently a struggle for life between a cat and a pigeon. So ends my little journey to Hythe".

"Back of Pipes" venue of Football on the Mud since 1965.

Back to 1964 and July 10 saw the re-instatement of the Football on the Mud fixture into the Hythe calendar. A match was played between teams of Hythe firemen and the Hythe Round Table. Colours, to start with, were white shirts, dark trousers and bow ties.

"The mud is looking beautiful and fit for the job," announced the commentator, as the match kicked off on a "pitch" to the north of Hythe Pier. A crowd of some 2000 people witnessed the spectacle, once featured in Pathe News, from the pier and shingle beach off West Street and saw the firemen romp home by five goals to one. Referee and local fishmonger Mr. John Madgewick, was at one time called upon to provide a rope in order to free a fireman stuck fast to his waist in the mud. After the match which realised £124 17s 5d for local charities, the victors paraded the "Mudlarkers Cup" in a lap of honour through the streets of Hythe before being hosed down by a fire appliance. Shortly afterwards the "pitch" was swallowed up by the Dibden Bay Reclaimation Scheme, a new and better one being found "Back of Pipes" south of Hythe Pier in time for the 1965 event.

Ferry skipper Mr. Fred Abrahams earnt himself a hero's tag during the evening of July 25, 1964. A 21 years old Southampton man fell from the gangway whilst landing at the Town Quay and being a non-swimmer found himself in immediate difficulties. Mr. Abrahams dived overboard and managed to keep him afloat by means of his hair, fixing a rope around him as he did so.

September 17, 1964 marked the retirement of 70 years old ferry skipper Capt. Wilf Banks of Jones Lane, Hythe. Capt. Banks had been working the passage since 1938 after a long and successful Merchant Navy career. Some of his wartime experiences were recorded in the local press the following day.

Capt. Banks told how the bombs nor blackout could deter him or his fellow skippers. As the bombs fell, they not only had to hope to escape a probable holocaust but had to avoid the numerous other small craft darting about lit only by the light from burning bomb damage. He recalled the remarkable mishap to the **Hotspur**, (of 1927), which under his command triggered off an accoustic mine, fortunately escaping with the minimum of harm.

The **Hotspur IV** was one of three vessels chartered by the Southampton Docks photographic and publicity staffs on June 27, 1965. She was employed along with the excursion vessels **Southampton Bell** and **Varos** to operate harbour cruises for over 700 persons, all of whom had converged on the port from camera clubs the width of Southern England. With equipment ranging from the inexpensive box to the sophisticated camera, the enthusiastic photographers took to the water on five cruises from 45 berth. Among the ocean liners on view were the **Canberra**, **Pretoria Castle**, **Reina Del Mar** and in dry-dock, the **Edinburgh Castle**. Ashore, pictures were being taken from every conceivable angle. Each of the guests was provided with a tea in the 45 berth canteen.

September 30, 1965 saw the retirement of Mr. Len Pearce after 38 years of employment by the General Estates Company. He had spent much of his career driving the pier train and had the honour of conversation with King George VI shortly prior to D.Day in 1944 during a Royal visit to Hythe Pier, the highlight of his career. To celebrate his retirement, his workmates presented the 72 year old with a clock.

After barely four decades passenger services on the Totton—Fawley Railway line were withdrawn on February 14. This young opposition which, at first more so than later, competed for the Southampton commuter traffic put further trade at the disposal of the ferry. Figures for 1966 are not available but with the motor vehicle bottleneck at the Totton Causeway "Y" Junction very much a contemporary problem, much of this floating traffic very likely took to the water.

Considerable pressure from local residents during the seventies to re-open the line was finally quashed in September 1975 when a British Rail report in which such a scheme was described as being "not a feasible project", was accepted by a Hampshire Planning and Transportation Committee. Instead, it was suggested that something be done to improve the ferry service and services "feeding" it.

Towards the end of 1965, the Southampton Sea Angling Club reported that fishing from Hythe Pier during the year had been at it's best since 1957. Perhaps some additional revenue from this disclosure was to be had from pier tolls during 1966.

In a television interview some years later, Commander J.D. Percy spoke of the displeasure he feels for gain from another's loss. It was impossible to avoid, however, during the 45 days shipping strike of May, June and July, 1966. People have always been attracted to Hythe Pier to view a passsing liner so when the opportunity arose to view as many as 25 at one time, as was the case when the strike finished on July 1, they arrived by the coachload. Other Hythe tradesmen didn't appear to share Commander Percy's scruples with one hotelier advertising an "unrivalled view". Whether Commander Percy approved or not it was nevertheless a profitable time as the Hythe Ferry with its non-union workforce was one of only a few shipping concerns operating throughout the entire nation. Even the Isle of Wight passage was redundant.

Like the seasonal harbour cruise propietors, the General Estates Company had at their disposal the best views to be had. The **Hotspur IV** carried a full compliment for almost all of her afternoon cruises whilst even the passage boats had much to offer the sightseer. On passage from Hythe they would pass, (on July 1), the **Chicanoa**, a Fyffes Line fruitship at Dockhead, the large passenger liners **Pendennis Castle** and **Caronia** lying at the Test Quays, the double banked **Roxburgh Castle** and **Rowallan Castle**, **Carmania** and **Port Lyttleton** and the magnificent **Queen Mary** all in the Ocean Dock, the Royal Mail Line's **Andes** in the Trafalgar Dry Dock and the Fyffes banana boats **Camito** and **Golfito** towering above the Town Quay landing steps as they lay just of the old Berth 50 Flying Boat Terminal.

Another attraction was the unique opportunity to perm the **Queen Elizabeth** and **Queen Mary** with either the **France** or **United States** and see three of the world's largest ocean liners in port together; once a common sight now a cherished memory. The grievances of the British seamen meant little to the thousands of sightseers, but were providing the greatest spectacle in Southampton's post war maritime history.

Shortly after the exodus of the strikebound ships, another occasion, on July 15, brought further visitors to Southampton's dockland and rivers. The occasion was that of the visit of Her Majesty Queen Elizabeth II to the new passenger terminal at berths 38 and 39 to perform the official opening ceremony. The ceremony was only a part of an exhaustive visit to the city but like the majority of vessels in the port, including the **Queen Elizabeth**, the "Hotspurs" were decorated with "Red Dusters" and "Union Jacks" for the occasion.

A very popular innovation during recent years had been the introduction of a quarter hour service during rush hours both morning and afternoon. The General Estates Company announced on September 16, 1966 that as from September 19 the afternoon quarter hour schedule between 4.30 and 5.30 would be extended to 6.30 p.m. A General Estates Company spokesman explained,
"Many office firms in Southampton are now working a five day week which means that many people do not finish work until 5.30 p.m. As they can get down to the Town Quay by 5.40 p.m. they at present have a twenty minute wait until 6.00 p.m. This extension of service should make travelling more comfortable and avoid people waiting".

During the foggy morning of November 24, 1966 the **Hotspur II** under the command of Mr. Stanley Renouf set out from Hythe Pier at 08.45 on a passage to the Town Quay that was more than just a little eventful. In short, the **Hotspur II** came within the bounds of a possible collision with the Cunard liner **Queen Mary** on her way out stern first from the Ocean Dock en route to New York. The incident with quotations from **Hotspur II** passengers made front page material for the local press but was in the words of the ferry skipper "grossly distorted". He complained to the newspaper who in turn allowed him his say by publishing his account on November 26. Mr. Renouf explained,
"On leaving Hythe, visibility was approximately half-a-mile and on approaching Hythe Knock Buoy, visibility deteriorated and it was then that the Harbour Patrol vessel came toward me to inquire whether a Control Officer was a passenger aboard my vessel.

On being informed that he was the patrol vessel accompanied the ferry toward Southampton. Off the Ocean Terminal the patrol boat informed me that the **Queen Mary** was backing out, and on sighting her I immediately stopped my vessel, turned her round some 1200 feet away and navigated round the stern of the **Queen Mary.**

The distance of 1200 feet (two cables) was confirmed by the radar on the Harbour Patrol boat".

In an issue of the Southern Evening Echo, on December 30,1966, ALW wrote in his "Along the Waterside" feature,
"As this is the time of year for taking a long look at the future I have consulted various local experts, and with help am able to bring all readers a highly unlikely peep into 1967". Regarding the Hythe Ferry he continued,
"During October Hythe Ferry switches over to a complete hovercraft service".

The main story of the winter of 1966—67 was not the perennial fogs but one of flooding. Persistant flooding of the Hythe village proper during a wet but hardly monsoon season made using the facilities provided by the General Estates and Hythe Pier companies somewhat uncomfortable.

Torrential rain fell during the afternoon and evening of October 22, 1966, flooding the High Street and The Marsh to depths of 24 and 12 inches respectively. The majority of shops in the affected area suffered structural and stock damage; the worst affected being Bell's Furnishing Stores of the High Street. Mr. Ronald Longman's photography shop in The Marsh was also particularly unfortunate.

Many ferry passengers partook in a little additional boat journey by being assisted to and from the safe retreat of Hythe Pier by Mr.Leslie Fry in his row-boat. Mrs. E. Pusey whose house in The Marsh was flooded after a passing bus had created a wave strong enough to force open her front door is on record for having said,

"It's the worst flooding I can remember in the village in the 58 years I have lived at this house".

Severe criticism of the village drainage was raised as the flooding occured with the tide at it's ebb. At a subsequent meeting of the Dibden Parish Council, a flood protection scheme was presented and approved, subject to Ministry approval. In the meantime temporary first-aid measures were put into effect but while these were still in hand further flooding was experienced. General Estates Company employee Mr. Harry Banks raised a flood warning early on January 26, 1967 as he saw the high tide reaching danger level following heavy overnight rain. Once informed, the local constabulary promptly raised shopkeepers to prepare their flood barriers but even so considerable stock damage was inflicted upon those unfortunate enough to miss the alarm. Ultimately water of some eighteen inches in depth covered the High Street, Prospect Place and The Marsh, causing severe discomfort to the ferry traffic.

One businessman whose premises in The Marsh were of the worst effected is on record as saying,

"We've got a pantomine coming off in Hythe, but this continual flooding of the village and the inability of the local council to stop it is the biggest pantomine of all".

Tempers were already frayed when yet further flooding, this time only of an inch or two, occured on February 20, 1967. Following a day of heavy rain the barricades were all in place in preparation for the evening's high tide at shop closing time but fortunately with the rain stopping just as the tide reached it's peak the only inconvenience caused was that to the ferry traffic. The following day, Army frogmen discovered the probable cause of the winter's troubles — three oil drums and a five foot railway sleeper lodged in a culvert beneath The Marsh. This blockage once cleared eased the situation considerably for on February 27 a heavy downpour was able to flow swiftly away. On the same day near hurricane force winds made the crossing of the passage somewhat turbulent, but the boats, crews and passengers weathered the storm.

Details of a £77,000 Flood Protection Scheme were announced in April 1967, and promptly executed, although not quite in time to prevent several inches of floodwater forming in the High Street, Prospect Place, The Marsh and parts of St. John's Street on October 4, 1967. Conditions were abnormal, however, with gale force eleven winds battering the district and torrential rain throughout the day.

The restaurant on the Hythe pierhead was broken into over the weekend of June 17 and 18, 1967. It was not until the proprietors, Messrs. B&H Caterers Ltd., opened for business during the morning of June 19 before the theft of five bottles of spirits to the value of £8. 10s. was discovered. A series of similar petty crimes were to be committed over the following months climaxing on August 8, 1968 when for the third time in little more than a week thieves struck with vengeance. On that occasion 1500 cigarettes and £5 cash was taken from the pierhead cafe and a radio and camera from the two ferry boats moored alongside the pier pontoon. Damage was also caused as all three casualties had to be entered forcibly. Such events were to be contributory factors in the decision to close Hythe Pier, at selected times, taken some years later.

The 1967 flooding was nothing new as this 1930's picture shows.

August 11, 1967 was a melancholy day for the older hands working the passage. Mr. William Arthur Lane died peacefully in Hythe Hospital at the age of 83. Mr. Lane, had retired upon Mr. J.G. Finlay's resumption of duties as General Manager after the Second World War. He had been appointed to the post in 1940, when Mr. Finlay joined up, having begun his career as a marine engineer in the days of the first **Hotspur** and the **Hampton**.

His greatest achievements were to follow, during the war years. Despite the harrowing conditions he kept the "Hotspurs" in service during the times when supplies of consumables and spare parts were difficult, sometimes impossible, to obtain. The secret visit of King George VI in 1944 needed the most sincere assistance from Mr. Lane; his staff being void of any knowledge of the event being a suitable tribute to his confidence. He went on to complete a half century of service to the General Estates Company.

"Hythe Pier and the foreshore at Hythe was thronged with people" the local press recorded on October 31, 1967, for the final departure of the famous Cunard liner **Queen Mary**. The scenes were very moving with hundreds of small boats escorting the liner out of port and an estimated 10,000 people watching from various points along Southampton Water, including the retainer banks of the Dibden Bay Reclaimation Scheme. Hythe Pier was packed to capacity making life very difficult for the ferry traffic having to continue throughout the proceedings. The ferries on passage as the mighty Queen approached Hythe Pier carried full complements and still left many disappointed persons shorebound.

Although a very sad day for the nation's shipping enthusiasts it was a profitable one for the General Estates and Hythe Pier companies, with a new crowd-pulling Queen just over the horizon.

After 57 years of employment by the General Estates Company, Mr. R. Brooks retired on December 8 at the age of 76. Mr. Brooks had joined the company in 1910 as a toll collector at an indoor market in Ilfracombe. He moved to Hythe shortly after the First World War. During the course of the Second World War he was appointed workshop foreman, holding the position till retirement. A presentation ceremony was held in the presence of Commander J.D. Percy and Mr. J.G. Finlay, the latter presenting Mr. Brooks with a watch and cigarette lighter subscribed for by his colleagues. In thanking Mr. Finlay, Commander Percy and his workmates, Mr. Brooks announced,
"I'm going to take things quietly now".

If Mr. J.G. Finlay, the General Manager of the General Estates Company, had ideas about a quiet retirement, it wasn't to be. Mr. Finlay who joined the company with managerial status in 1936 spent the final six months of his career grooming a successor, only to find himself back in harness little more than a year later.

After 26 years service, (not including the years spent on war duty), Mr. Finlay retired at the beginning of April 1968. He was always a sincere man and became very popular with his workforce right from the start. In November 1967 Mr. John "Jack" Wright had been engaged by the General Estates Company to work alongside until and succeed upon the retirement of Mr. Finlay. A party was held to toast the retirement and was attended by many of his colleagues including Mr. Wright and Commander J.D. Percy. The room was decorated in the manner of a ship's wheelhouse with a central table draped with a "Union Jack" and sporting a ship's wheel.

Following the resignation, for personal reasons, of Mr. Wright, Mr. Finlay's reinstatement was intended to be shortlived, the company proving their word by announcing in May 1969 the appointment of Mr. R.R.J. Morgan to take affect from October of the same year. Mr. Finlay was finally able to retire in November 1969. Sadly, the hard earnt retirement was to be short, for he died in March 1971.

Mr. Morgan was well known and respected in the village being a member of the local constabulary. Although christened with the names Robert Richard James and known to his family as Jim, throughout his police force career he was always called Tim. The name, which he couldn't leave behind in the old New Road Police Station, came about as a result of there already being a Tim Morgan at Romsey, where he began his career as an eighteen year old constable in 1939. To avoid confusion the nicknames "old Tim" and "young Tim" were adopted, young Tim's following him through his career. After his contribution to the war effort, in which his naval service saw him involved with allied landings in the South of France, Sicily and Yugoslavia, he was deployed to Ringwood and engaged on CID work, being promoted to Sargeant in 1954. Following further postings he finally arrived at Hythe where he was promoted to Inspector in 1961. In 1968 he achieved the rank of Chief Inspector before retirement from the force at the end of June 1969 following 30 years of service.

Back to 1968, when on April 27 the 09.30 a.m. ferry boat from Hythe had aboard, perhaps, it's most unusual cargo for many years. A mobile bath fitted with wheels and accompanied by about a dozen pupils from the Hardley Secondary School, "sailed" across the passage as part of an advertising campaign for the Hardley May Fair scheduled for May 4. The pupils and bath returned to Hythe on the same ferry boat at 10.00 a.m. and on both crossings distributed handbills advertising the event from which the proceeds were to be donated to the Hardley Secondary School swimming pool project.

Once again on June 30, 1968 the **Hotspur IV** was employed to operate two harbour cruises for 350 camera club members on a visit to Southampton Docks. Shortly afterwards she was brought alongside the old Hythe Quay to undergo extensive propulsion and some structural alterations. A few months later, the **Hotspur IV** was re-commissioned with new T4 Kelvin diesel engines, bridge controlled and slender twin uptakes, replacing her original single funnel, aft of her engine room cover. Similar alterations were made to the **Hotspur III** in 1969, but she retained her single funnel and received Kelvin R6 diesels.

As the decade came to a close Hythe still had much to offer, not the least being an unequalled view of the maiden arrival of the new ocean liner **Queen Elizabeth2** on December 19, 1968. The General Estates Company expected to be very busy and made extensive preparations for the arrival including additional overtime for several of their staff. The **Queen Elizabeth 2** departed early afterwards on a trials cruise, it will be recalled, only to limp pathetically back into Southampton on January 2, 1969 and thus delay the really big occasion, the maiden voyage. The "big occasion" took place on May 2, 1969 and it was not only extra staff required that day; over 400 pier tickets had been issued for the occasion of the departure of the liner

Reconstructed Hotspur IV on cruise during the late 1960's.

for a second trial cruise a fortnight previous; additional police personnel were requisitioned too. The crowds assembled throughout the morning with the excitement growing by the minute as the 12.30 p.m. departure time drew closer. A coachload of London schoolchildren arrived, bringing with them their own brand of excitement. As a thousand coloured balloons were released over the Ocean Dock to herald the departure, the Hythe pierhead, decorated with flags and bunting, exploded into life. Excitement bubbled over as the cheers of the 3000 persons watching from the Ocean Terminal building and the thousands more from adjacent quays were echoed from Hythe Pier and echoed again by the multitudes watching from both shores the length of Southampton Water. There were hundreds of small boats, including the **Hotspur IV** on a special excursion, fireboats spraying water into the air, helicopters and an RAF fly-past. It was a very special day. The **Queen Elizabeth 2** was quickly forgiven for her inauspicious start and accepted with the affection afforded her stately predeccessors. The General Estates Company could bank on her to draw crowds whenever in port and even more so when on the move. Proof of this was to be had on August 20, 1969. Even though it was a Wednesday and early closing for the village shops, with both the **Queen Elizabeth 2** and the **United States** passing Hythe Pier that afternoon, the pier and ferries were descended upon by multitudes of holiday makers. During the early afternoon traffic "moving" into Hythe tailed back the length of both Jones Lane and West Street.

During the preceeding winter a survey of Hythe—Southampton ferry traffic was conducted on December 10, 1968 by the County Planning Office. A questionaire was handed to each person passing through the Hythe Pier entrance and onto the Town Quay landing steps. Among the questions asked were the purpose of crossing the passage and the means of conveyance to and from the ferry.

At a meeting of the Dibden Parish Council on December 16, it was reported that on a recent occasion Hythe based football supporters had found themselves fogbound in Southampton as, due to the conditions, the Hythe ferry boats were unable to operate. This was not a unique situation, but concern for the number of schoolboys who had found themselves seeking alternate transport home having already exhausted their money upon the purchase of return tickets at Hythe was expressed. The meeting agreed that the General Estates Company be approached on the possibility of refunding amounts for the return portion of tickets whenever the conditions prevented the company from executing their commitments. The General Estates Company's reply was read at a meeting of the Council on January 20, 1969. The ferry proprietors naturally regretted the inconvenience caused by the cancelled services but rendered it impossible to refund monies on return tickets. However, in the near future, in accordance with national trends, it was intended to abolish the return ticket and issue single journey tickets at a slightly reduced price.

Abolition of the concessionary return, came into effect with an increase in fares on May 11, 1969, although return tickets were still available at no advantage until January 4, 1971. However, by request it is still possible even today to purchase return tickets in the manner of two singles, one rubber stamped with the letter "R". The new fares were 1s 10d single, 3s 8d return.

After many years of minimal involvement, the Dibden Parish Council seemed to be finding themselves much concerned in the affairs of the Hythe—Southampton passage during the late sixties and into the early seventies. On June 8, 1970 they discussed a communication from the Fawley Parish Council informing the recipients of a request from a Fawley parishioner to have a late ferry service, particularly on Friday and Saturday when the younger generation sought entertainment in Southampton, often till, say, 01.30 a.m. It was resolved to invite comments on the practicability of such a service from both the General Estates Company and the Hants and Dorset Motor Services Company, both replying as expected that it would be quite uneconomical.

Modern Times 1970-1986

On December 18, 1970 the General Estates Company had announced reductions in services to take effect from January 4, 1971. A company spokesman explained,
"For over 70 years this company has endeavoured to provide an efficient ferry service at low cost to the public, but rising costs have made it necessary for us to introduce economies to keep fares as far as possible at their present level".

The "economies" entailed the withdrawal of the quarter hourly schedule during the rush hours "because of a steady decline in use", with a return to the previous arrangement of a half-hourly schedule commencing from Hythe at 07.00 a.m. and from Southampton at 07.15 a.m. on weedays. There was also to be an hour long break between 8.00 p.m. and 9.00 p.m. from Hythe and 7.45 p.m. and 8.45 p.m. from Southampton during the weekday evenings. The Sunday programme was to be even more restricted with the total abandonment of services before 2.00 p.m. from Hythe, 2.15 p.m. from Southampton, when a half-hourly schedule would operate until 10.00 p.m. and 10.30 p.m., respectively.

There was the expected criticism, albeit surprisingly subdued, but the company held firm, although it wasn't too long before the quarter-hourly rush hour boats were re-introduced.

A revised time table was issued as follows on January 3, 1972.

Ferry Time Table

3rd Jan, 1972 until further notice

Weekday half-hourly Service

Boats leave HYTHE	Boats leave SO'TON (Town Quay)
7.0 am	7.15 am
and every half-hour until 8.0 pm then 9.0 pm and every half hour until 10.30 pm	and every half-hour until 7.45 pm then 8.45 pm and every half hour until 10.45 pm
Mon. to Fri.	Mon. to Fri.

ADDITIONAL BOATS

7.45 am	8 am
8.15 am	8.30 am
4.45 pm	5 pm

Sunday Service

HYTHE	SO'TON (Town Quay)
2.00 pm then half-hourly until 8 pm and at 9 pm & 10 pm	2.15 pm then half-hourly until 8.30 pm and at 9.30 & 10.30 pm

Subject to alteration

THE PIER TRAIN will be FREE for passengers using the ferry, when seats are available

Fare:

Adult 12p Child (under 14) 7p

The Hythe and Southampton Ferry Service will be maintained at the times advertised, unless prevented by fog, tempest, stoppage by harbour authorities, accidents, contingencies and the like.
THE GENERAL ESTATES CO. LTD. Hotspur House. Hythe, Southampton. Tel. HYTHE 3203

Ferry Timetable

Commander J.D. Percy announced still further cuts on December 8, 1972. It was intended to cancel all services after 8.00 p.m. every evening and the Sunday schedule in total as from January 1, 1973 with a restricted Sunday service during the summer months. Commander Percy explained,

"During the winter it is costing us £100 a night in wages to run after 8.00 p.m. and we are only getting £30 of this back in fares. This is intolerable and the only alternative we have to cover the loss is to severely raise the fares. This of course, will affect our regular commuters whom we try to look after. In fact we will be giving the public an improved service because we will be able to run two extra ferries between 5.00 p.m. and 6.00 p.m.".

Clearly, such drastic measures were to face stiff opposition. Although not announced publicly until December 8 the Dibden Parish Council had got wind of them a few days earlier as at a meeting on December 4 concern was expressed about the matter. A letter to the council from Mr. R.R.J. Morgan giving details of the aforementioned cuts was read. Mr. Morgan explained that while the General Estates Company realised that as in all forms of public transport they were expected to subsidise those lesser so by their better patronised services, there had to be a limit. As the result of a two month survey at a favourable period earlier in the year, the aforementioned services being beyond this limit it was proposed, with regret, to dispence with them. By doing so it enabled the company to retain the fares at their then present level. The mood of the meeting was one of apathy and so it was moved to write to the General Estates Company asking them to reconsider and further to request the details of the survey.

At a subsequent meeting of the Dibden Parish Council on December 11 the councillors inspected the figures, so promptly supplied by Mr. Morgan, and concluded, albeit reluctantly, that the General Estates Company were correct with their conclusion that the pending curtailment of services was fully justified on the grounds of economy.

In every final undertaking there is nostalgia of bygone and often better times. It was so of the last "last boat" from Southampton, which over the years had become something of an institution. On December 30, 1972, a minute or two late, the 10.45 p.m. left the Town Quay with the last of the inevitable late-comers safely aboard following the traditional High Street dash.

Although the cuts were made with the commuter's interests in mind, the non-existence of evening services regretably drove much of the casual traffic to the private motor car, as with Mr. Sam D. Kingdon, a Hythe resident, who in a letter to the Southern Evening Echo early in 1974 described the revised schedule as "a service worse now than ever before". Mr. Kingdon was certainly not alone with his views. Indeed, he could find some sympathy with even the ferry proprietors themselves, but the subsequent quadrupling of oil prices pushed any re-instatement of these services well and truly beyond the point of no return.

"In January I expect the local sailing club to take over running the late night ferry services between Southampton and Hythe" predicted a local newspaper columnist on January 5, 1973. A little sarcastic perhaps, but those long ago almost forgotten days of the wherrymen would have been welcomed back with open arms by many a would be traveller.

Incident was notable for it's absence during the opening years of the new decade. One occasion, however, was on May 4, 1971 when a young girl boarding the **Hotspur III** slipped and fell from the gangway into the water. She was promptly brought onto the pier pontoon and although no worse than a little shocked sent to Hythe Hospital as a precaution.

After more than two centuries a family tradition was broken on November 8, 1972. There had been a "Banks" connected with the Hythe—Southampton passage for all of this time but on his seventieth birthday Mr. Harry Banks, became the most recent and possibly the last member of the family to retire from it's employment. Reference has already been made to his father, Henry Thomas Banks, but before him there had been his grandfather, Jack Banks, and great-grandfather, Richard "Dickie" Banks, who witnessed the earliest Hythe steamers. Harry Banks had been working on the ferry boats since he was a boy of eight and once achieving regular employment quickly climbed the ranks to skipper. A presentation of gifts including a compass from his friends and colleagues was made by Commander J.D. Percy, who in a short speech summed up the Banks connection by saying,
"this is a day he has to share with his ancestors."

Another long established employee retired on January 5, 1973. He was Mr. Robert "Roy" Davis, who had driven the Hythe Pier train for some 27 years. He acquired his nickname at school, since when very few people have known it to be anything other than his mother's choice. He joined the General Estates Company in 1945 after a year convalescing a serious wound received during service with the Royal Artillery in France. Before the Second World War he was a gardener, having been employed at three of the local mansions, Mount House, West Cliff Hall and Langdown House respectively. At a presentation to mark the retirement, Mr. Davis received a pipe and an alarm clock from the General Estates Company's yard bosun, Mr. Frederick Abrahams. With respect to all those who have driven the train since January 5, 1973, the train without "Roy" Davis has been like a Monday or Wednesday evening without Coronation Street, bacon without eggs or any other institution one cares to mention. His undefinable popularity was perpetuated in a portrait, subsequently hung in the Ferry Bar of the Lord Nelson public house.

The Hythe Pier train was at the centre of a controversy during the summer of 1973 and again during that of 1974. It all stemmed from a decision taken by the General Estates Company that as the fare for train passage along the pier had been incorporated into that for the ferry passage some eighteen months previous, to avoid the problems experienced during the summer of 1972 the train would be for the use of the ferry traffic only, a notice to this effect being placed on the notice board at the pier entrance. While resolving the problem of ferry passengers not being able to find a seat on the train and thus, sometimes, missing ferry boat departures, it produced another, the much valued sightseeing business being denied use of some of the available facilities.

At a meeting of the Dibden Parish Council on September 3, 1973, concern was expressed that elderly people were being denied pleasure of viewing shipping from the Hythe pierhead owing to the General Estates Company's ruling and representations to the pier proprietors on this matter were urged. This was done and at a subsequent meeting on September 10, the clerk, reported upon the proceedings. Mr. R.R.J. Morgan had explained, on behalf of the General Estates Company, that the ruling was only of a temporary nature during the busiest months of the year, July and August, when pier promenaders often overloaded the train at the expense of the ferry traffic, even with additional journeys available. Regarding elderly folk, the company sympathised to the extent of issuing instructions to their drivers to use their discretion. The meeting resolved to urge alternate arrangements for the summer of 1974. Mr. Morgan's reply to the resolution was read at a meeting on October 8. His doubt as to whether an alternate scheme would be any more practical was not met too favourably, but it was resolved to adjourn the case until the following spring. The dispute was resurected in May 1974 when it was reported at a meeting of the Dibden Parish Council on the 20th. that an elderly lady after having paid her pier toll was refused transportation to the pierhead on a comparitively empty train as her intention was merely to view the shipping and not to use the ferry. It was resolved that the General Estates Company be reminded of their instructions to their train drivers.

A written apology from Mr. Morgan regarding the incident was submitted at a meeting of the Council on June 10, 1974. Mr. Morgan added that his train drivers had been instructed that whenever possible elderly people were to be conveyed along the pier even if they were not ferry passengers. However, reference to a notice at the pier entrance which stated that only ferry passengers were entitled to use the train was raised in the chamber. This, it was felt, would deter elderly people from even aproaching the train driver. It was therefore resolved to request the General Estates Company to add to the notice that elderly people could be conveyed during quiet periods.

***Hotspur IV** after addition of stern canopy pictured in 1973. (Alan Titheridge)*

At the next meeting on July 8, 1974, a further letter from Mr. Morgan was read and discussed. The notice, said Mr. Morgan, was essential, particularly at the seaward end of the pier where ferry passengers arrived from Southampton en bloc. However, he conceded that there were times when the notice could be withdrawn and further informed the Dibden Parish Council that he had again reminded his train drivers to use their utmost descretion regarding all pier promenaders.

It would appear that the notice at the pier entrance remained without the suggested clause and so it was resolved to request the clerk, Mrs. Jean Sizer, to include in her monthly newspaper column in the Forest and Waterside Observer with Totton Times reference to Mr. Morgan's instruction to his train drivers.

The August 1974 edition carried the following entry,

> "The Hythe and Southampton Ferry Co. has found it necessary again to restrict the use of the train at Hythe Pier for ferry passengers only during busy periods such as commuter times and during the summer when there is a large influx of holiday makers. The company has stated however, that elderly people who are not ferry passengers will be conveyed on the train if they inform the driver that they would like to go to the end of the pier."

As the dispute progressed the train continued to journey the length of Hythe Pier, many, many times daily, except for a short while during the wet and blustery day of October 16, 1973.

A day or two previous, work had commenced on relaying the shore end section of the track. A temporary buffer was placed a little further along the line. During the rush hour period the train skidded on the slippery rails as it braked towards the new teminal point, careering into the temporary buffer. After a swift precautionary inspection normal operations were resumed.

March 11, 1974 had seen the publication of a new time table and an increase in fares. The new tariffs were to be as follows, adult single, 14p., child single, 9p, bicycle, perambulator or dog, 9p, and pier toll, 3p. The time table showed ferry boats leaving Hythe Pier and the Town Quay at half-hour intervals from 07.00 a.m. till 7.30 p.m. and 07.15 a.m. till 7.45 a.m. respectively. Additional sailings were also available, from Hythe at 07.45, 08.15 and 08.45 a.m., 4.45 and 5.15 p.m. and from Southampton at 08.00, 08.30 and 09.00 a.m., 5.00 and 5.30 p.m. A restricted Sunday service was to be implemented.

Reference has already been made to the closure of Hythe Pier during the hours of darkness and to some of the earlier reasons behind the unavoidable decision and it's execution. Things were really brought to a head during the early-middle seventies when among the abuses of trust committed were lighting of fires on the pier decking, extinction of the pier's navigation lights, forced entry into and theft from the pierhead cafe, restaurant, coin operated telescopes and ferry boats, vandalism to pierhead buildings and toilets and the cutting off of the pier water supply.

Commander J.D. Percy announced on May 31, 1974 that the pier was to be closed between 10.00 p.m. and 6.30 a.m. daily "as soon as contact had been made with the interested authorities." The decision was much regretted by Commander Percy but, with apologies to the angling fraternity, "in the interest of preventing more serious damage and consequent impairment of the ferry service this step had to be taken." It came into effect on July 1, 1974 and was subsequently extended to an 8.00 p.m. closure.

As with many occasions over the years the Dibden Parish Council had the question of bus and ferry time-tables not being in harmony on their agenda when they met on April 21, 1975. They discussed a copy of a letter from the Windmill Copse Residents Association (Hythe) to the Hants and Dorset Motor Services Ltd. regarding the non-connection of their Hythe—Lymington services with the ferry. However, the meeting was reminded of their previous involvement and opinion was expressed that so long as the two concerns competed for business it was quite unreasonable to expect them to connect their timings.

Ferry passengers had to be at Hythe Pier in good time on May 10, 1975 owing to the train being out of action due to troubles with the rectifiers. It wasn't until late on May 12 before the train could be put back on service. Fortunately the tenth and eleventh constituted a week-end, thereby only the early morning commuters on May 12 being inconvenienced to any extent, even then it was a dry and pleasant day. This was not so on October 24, 1975, however, when the train suffered the ignominy of similar trouble. Same day repairs were possible but not until after the early morning commuters had had to walk the pier and wait for the foggy conditions to improve before passage was possible. The **Hotspur III** did manage the 07.30 a.m. crossing to the Town Quay, to be followed by the **Hotspur IV** at 07.55 a.m. only to be stranded in Southampton until 08.45 a.m. and 08.30 a.m. respectively.

Fog further disrupted the schedules during the mornings of September 8 and October 29, 1975 and the evening of December 20, 1975. The occasion of September 8 was further troubled with a grounding of the **Hotspur III**.

The ferry boat set out from Hythe Pier at 07.10 a.m. with 32 passengers aboard. The fog, fairly dense but navigatable, quickly thickened. As the vessel edged her way through the fog she suddenly came to a halt, having run aground between North West Netley and the Weston Shelf. The **Hotspur III** found herself in this opposite direction to the regular passage due to a technical fault with her magnetic compass, but after a few minutes full astern managed to free herself. During this time the engineer kept a watchful eye on the engine gauges as the temperatures rose while the crewman reassured the passengers. The **Hotspur III** eventually arrived at the Town Quay at about 07.35 a.m. some twenty minutes late.

The **Hotspur III** was involved in another, horrific, incident on October 27, 1975. As a result, a thirteen years old schoolgirl had to be rushed to hospital for an emergency operation to repair organic injuries.

Witnesses have explained how as the **Hotspur III** started to pull away from the Town Quay landing steps, a mooring rope still connected with the quayside stretched to the limit when suddenly the ironwork of the quayside came away, the whiplash plunging it into the young lady's back. Other witnesses have told how the mate was impeded in executing his duty of undoing the mooring rope by passengers standing in his way. Whilst the 4.45 p.m. was crowded it was no more so than for any other commuter time departure, although, perhaps, too many were in the wrong place at the wrong time. Obviously the young lady took the brunt of the whiplash but one or two other passengers and the mate and Town Quay porter also received minor injuries. The Department of the Environment and Harbour Authority subsequently made enquiries. The General Estates Company, too, instigated an immediate private investigation. However, Mr. R.R.J. Morgan did have to say for the ferry proprietors,

"It appears the metal hook on the pile on the Town Quay steps, to which the eye of the rope was attached, gave way causing the rope and hook to fly through the air."

It was revealed during mid December, 1975 that the New Forest District Council had agreed in principal to impose charges on their Waterside area car parks to take effect as from the summer of 1976.

One advantage of the hitherto free parking at the Hythe car parks in New Road and Jones Lane was that motorists could leave their cars and proceed to Southampton by ferry, thus avoiding the not inexpensive fees for car parking in the city, with ferry fares costing little, if any, more than the petrol needed to journey there by road.

With this in mind a subsequent decision was taken not to impose a toll on the Jones Lane car park. However, a scheme for a "park and ride" ticket was thought desirable in the council chambers. The parking charges were never implemented.

Further bringing of the story of the Hythe Ferry up to date necessitates, first, looking back to "ancient times". It will be recalled that the earliest reference to a ferry at Hythe is the legend "Hitheferye" on Saxton's 1575 Map of Hampshire, 400 years previous. To celebrate this fact an open day was held on May 31, 1975, a day which in itself had no significance nor any particular reason for having been

May 31 1975, the "400th anniversary" celebrations (all pictures Alan Titheridge)

chosen but turned out to be something very special.

Commander J.D. Percy appeared in a short feature on BBC Television's Friday edition of their "Nationwide" programme, the day previous, and did as much to promote the ferry as any had done before him. Take your children on a short sea cruise, suggested the presenter, there'll be no charges, tomorrow. There were to be none either. No passports required, he quipped in conclusion. But Hythe still is an unknown quantity to many on the eastern side of Southampton Water.

May 31, 1975 began with clear blue skies but although warm, it was clear that mid summer was a month or two away. The **Hotspur III** opened the proceedings at 07.00 a.m. plying half-hourly to and from the Town Quay until joined by the **Hotspur II** at 09.15 a.m. when a quarter-hourly schedule was put into operation.

It was about this time that those unfortunate enough to have to work on Saturday mornings made way for the Saturday morning shoppers. Together with those simply making an outing of it, they produced a response beyond all expectations, prompting Mr. R.R.J. Morgan to comment,
"such were the numbers that we had to keep up a shuttle service and this continued until late evening. It was very gratifying".

Indeed, but for the two hour break mid day to nourish the crews, the quarter-hourly schedule had to be maintained almost throughout the day. It had been a very long time since the **Hotspur II** had piled the passage with anything like a full complement of passengers but under the command of skipper Mr. R. McCully she left the Town Quay Pontoon at 1.00 p.m. with 298 persons aboard, just two short of her licenced capacity. The Town Quay Pontoon had to be used so as to be able to employ two gangways, only one being possible at the regular landing steps, thus gaining greater mobility in passenger movement.

The "Hotspurs", flying the "red duster" from their sterns and bunting from their masts were a picture, as, indeed, was the colourful flag draped pier-head. One could almost forget it was 1975 and imagine the regatta days of the turn of the century. The Hythe Pier entrance, too, was gaily decorated and the train operated almost without a pause.

Without a doubt the celebrations were an enormous success. In all, 7678 single journies were recorded.

1976 was a very eventful year. As early as March 8 things started to happen when owing to mechanical troubles the Hythe Pier train was put out of action just after 6.00 p.m.

On March 29, the early morning "rush hour" was thrown into total disarray as the **Hotspur III** had been found to be taking in water by the crew setting about preparing her for service prior to the day's first departure at 06.00 a.m. With the **Hotspur IV** being overhauled on the mud close by the Hythe Pier entrance the older, slower **Hotspur II** became the only vessel available and ran with a near full passenger complement for each Southampton bound passage between 07.30 and 09.30 a.m.

Some thirty inches of Water had collected in the **Hotspur III**'s engine room between the time she moored alongside the pierhed pontoon on Saturday (March 27) evening and the time of it's discovery. Mr R.R.J. Morgan explained to the local press that after the engine room had been pumped out the leak was found to be through a stern tube mechanical failure.

On April 7 it was trouble again for the train, when owing to a points failure at the shore end of the railway track it spectacularly jack-knifed when approaching the sheds, causing damage to both track and coach bogies. The train had been along the pier, without passengers, to deliver the fuel tanker. However, some inconvenience was caused as the accident put the train out of commission for several hours.

Whilst peering from a window in his Hotspur House flat during the evening of August 4 Commander Percy observed signs of a fire a little more than half way along the length of Hythe Pier. He promptly raised an alarm bringing three fire appliances from Hythe and a fireboat from Southampton to the incident. Firemen had to rip up planks to prevent the fire spreading and to get at the flames spouting from a timber bearer below. These were also being attended by the fireboat beneath.

It is thought that the fire was started by a lighted cigarette, thoughtlessly dicarded, and fanned up by wind. Company workmen completed repairs the following morning causing minimal inconvenience to foot passengers and none at all to the train and ferry boats, which we able to operate to schedule.

September 16 saw the sad death of Commander J.D. Percy, who had been at the head of the General Estates Company since the death of his father in 1936. Commander Percy was born on October 9, 1913 at Ealing in West London where he attended a local day school. From there he went to Oundle School, Northamptonshire on the engineering side and after leaving school he went to Faraday House, the Institution of Electrical Engineers. Then followed a year's apprenticeship at Tangye's works in the Midlands and a year's employment with a French electrical construction company at Nancy in north west France, which ended when he joined the family concern.

Commander Percy's distinguished wartime career has already been detailed in ealier pages. After the war he resumed control of the business and was appointed to the Hythe Bench in 1950 and served a total of 26 years as magistrate. The funeral took place at St. Andrews Church, Dibden Purlieu on September 23. Following Commander Percy's death Mr. T.M. Percy was appointed Chairman and Managing Director, but Commander Percy's son-in-law, Mr. P.F. Walker, who had been appointed a director in 1975, assumed responsibility for the direction of the ferries.

On November 1, a new company was formed to use the existing buildings at the Hythe pierhead primarily as an aquarium, but also to exhibit subjects related to local history as well as providing catering facilities. The company, Marine Life Resources Ltd. in subsequent words of new General Estates Company chairman Mr. T.M. Percy, "didn't really get off the ground".

Early in November a number of further developments were announced. These entailed the installation of radar on the **Hotspur IV**, re-springing of the Pier Train rolling stock and proposals for a new ferry boat to replace the aging **Hotspur II**. On the latter Mr. T.M. Percy is quoted as saying at the time, "plans are at the drawing board stage for an aluminium catamaran type of ferry. Nothing has definately been decided yet, but if we go ahead the new craft could be in service in 1978".

Since the very first of the steamers, operations have been disrupted whenever fog descended over the passage. The installation of radar into the **Hotspur IV** during November 1976 put an end to all that. The system fitted was a Seascan which has a range of 16 nautical miles.

As from February 1, 1977 the operation of the Hythe Ferry and Hotspur cruises has been operated by Southern Coastcrafts Ltd., formed to control both the General Estates Company's Hythe boats and its East Anglian interests. The latter includes a ferry across the River Yare at Great Yarmouth and the Yarmouth & Gorleston Steamboat Co. Ltd., who own and operate the **Norwich Belle** on sea trips and the **Broadland Belle** on the Broads.

At about this time decisions were made to procede with the new ferry at Hythe. An order was placed with Marine Services Ltd. of Hythe during the Autumn of 1977 and on an advance of monies preparatory works were put into effect. However, things were not to go according to plan. On December 23 the shipyard proprietors announced that their bankers had refused further credit and frozen their assets and that a liquidator was about to be appointed. The company couldn't even pay their 20 strong workforce, who had to face Christmas "on the dole".

"It came out of the blue" Mr T.M. Percy told the contemporary press. "Work has begun on the ferry and advance payment has been made by us to MSL and we hope a liquidator with confidence could still back them".

It wasn't to be.

Meanwhile, back on the passage, the **Hotspur III** became involved in a rescue during the stormy evening of November 14, 1977. While on passage, skipper Mr. Alan Reynolds picked up distress calls on his vessel's radio from a man drifting helplessly in a launch. Gale force winds prevented the prospect of getting a line aboard the vessel which had broken from its moorings, so the **Hotspur III** moved closer so that her mate, Mr. Fred Maidment, could jump aboard. This was accomplished, despite lashing waves, and as the **Hotspur III** proceded to Hythe without him the ferry crewman further managed to start the launch's engines and follow on.

The force 10 gales that night caused extensive damage to the pier. Corrugated sheets were ripped from the roof of the aged cafeteria and sections of the perspex canopy over the pierhead also fell to the decking. At one stage during the course of the early evening, plans were in hand to close the pier and abandon the remaining ferry operations.

Following the disappointment of the failure in building the new ferry boat, Mr. Peter Walker announced on April 28, 1978 that the General Estates Company had put in a bid for the Portsmouth based ferry **Southsea Queen**. The bid of £160,000 was successful and she arrived at Hythe on June 14.

Southsea Queen shortly after arrival at Hythe. (Alan Titheridge)

Although a certain amount of interior modifications were thought desirable, including the replacement of a lot of wooden seating, the **Southsea Queen** entered service in July. Her name was changed to **Hythe Hotspur** on September 25, 1978 and her colour scheme altered to it's present format in July 1979. When originally viewed by the General Estates Company's directors, the **Southsea Queen** had a lime green livery but appeared at Hythe painted white. The alterations thought desirable in the interest of passenger comfort were carried out during the winter of 1978—79.

The **Hythe Hotspur** was put into operation mainly on cruising and charter work, being used on the passage only when the **Hotspur III** and **Hotspur IV** were unavailable. Owing to her size the Harbour authorities permit use of the Town Quay pontoon whenever possible. Her registered owners are the General Estates Company although she is operated by Southern Coastcrafts Ltd.

The successful introduction of the **Hythe Hotspur** enabled the proposed withdrawal of the ageing **Hotspur II** to be put into effect. She was offered for sale and subsequently a bid of £27,000 was accepted from the Clyde Marine Motoring Company. The **Hotspur II**, renamed **Kenilworth**, arrived at Greenock on Scotland's River Clyde during mid March 1979 and was put into service on the Gourock — Kilcreggan passage on April 2.

The most recent addition to the General Estates fleet, Hythe Hotspur pictured in 1980. (Bill Jones)

The Greenock Telegraph reported on March 31, "the distance from Hythe to Southampton is exactly the same as the Gourock — Kilcreggan run and she will be the ideal vessel for the crossing".

During the following summer there was another fire scare on Hythe Pier, when the Pier train assumed the unlikely role of fire engine. As the train proceded down the Pier with its load of passengers for the ferry, flames were seen spouting from between the pier planking. Without waiting for passengers for the return trip the train swiftly departed to the incident. Driver Mr. Patrick Ford and ferry crewman Mr. Ernie Nutbeam armed with fire buckets, lowered them over the Pier by means of ropes to collect seawater to douse the flames. Mr. Ford was later reported as saying, "it was a cigarette end stuck in between the boards that started the fire".

1980 saw renewed interest in a new vessel for the Hythe — Southampton passage, which gathered momentum later in the year when problems arose with the **Hotspur III**. A dry inspection revealed major deterioration of the hull, by then 42 years old. The extensive repair work deemed necessary was considered uneconomical and so after her final passage on October 13, 1980 she was withdrawn. Demolition work was begun in February 1981 on the mud closeby the ferry yard and completed in early June. However, many of her fittings were preserved for use in the new ferry at the time in the latter stages of contractural preparation. The **Hotspur III**'s register was closed on March 12, 1981.

On April 23, 1981 the contract for the new ferry was placed with Arun Yacht and Boat Company Ltd. of Littlehampton, Sussex by the General Estates Company, who would own the new ferry which, like the **Hythe Hotspur**, will be operated by Southern Coastcrafts Ltd. The contract price for the new vessel was £96,950, not including the cost of windows, seats etc. A grant of 50% of the contract price, with a ceiling of £50,000, had been negotiated with the Hampshire County Council.

The new ferry was expected to be handed over in November but numerous problems with the builders delayed her launch until March 17, 1982 and arrival at Hythe until the following July. After being fitted out locally, bearing the name **New Forester** she slipped quietly and quite unceremoniously into service during the early morning rush hour on August 20, 1982.

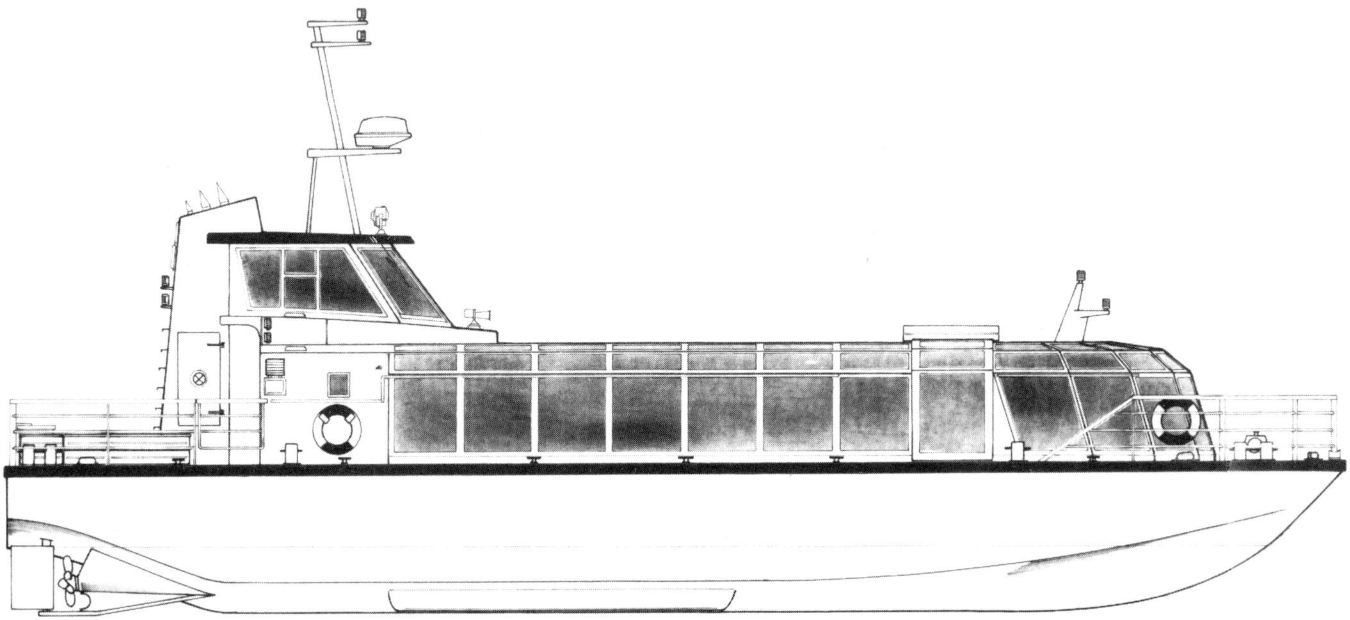

Artist's impression of new ferry due for completion November 1981.

An inauguration cruise from Hythe Pier was held at 11.00 a.m. on September 27, 1982 attended by several local dignitaries, directors and company staff. In his speech at the subsequent buffet lunch, the Chairman of the Hampshire County Council Public Transport sub-committee, Councillor Arthur Hill said,
"The County Council is deeply committed to public transport and one of the best ways we can pursue this policy is to assist the operators with getting on with the job. The Hythe Ferry provides a vital transport link and we will do everything we can to support private enterprise in this essential service".
Mr. Peter Walker, Managing Director of the General Estates Co., in his reply thanked those present before touching upon future hopes for the service.

The **New Forester** is quite different in design from any previous vessel on the passage. The bar and light refreshment facilities, upholstered seating and all round tinted panoramic windows make her a most pleasant vessel in which to travel and a boon to charter and cruising activites.

On July 21, 1981 there was an unfortunate incident aboard the **Hythe Hotspur** as she waited for passengers at the Town Quay. As sixty-eight years old Mrs. Gladys Angus lowered herself onto a bench seat on the outside deck, it collapsed under her, causing her to fall and hit her head against the vessel's rail. Contact was immediately made with Hythe, where an ambulance awaited the arrival of the **Hythe Hotspur** in order to convey the Holbury woman to Hythe Hospital. Mrs. Angus was not detained after treatment.

Mr. Tim Morgan, manager of Southern Coastcrafts, said after the incident,
"It's certainly very unfortunate for the lady concerned and I am looking into the reasons for it".

Modern Wheelhouse

NEW FORESTER

Modern Interior

In an age before modern Leisure Centres the pier was a good place for diving.

Investigations were put into immediate effect and blame was credited to the plague of modern society, vandalism.

"For some reason" Mr. Morgan announced, "these people get a kick out of removing the screws which anchor the chair legs to the floor. It's been a problem for some time on the lower deck, despite extra staff supervision, but now it seems to be spreading upstairs. Our shipwrights regularly inspect the anchoring and replace broken screws and our staff are also constantly on the watch for anyone tampering with the fittings".

The **Hythe Hotspur** again featured in the headlines for the wrong reasons after an incident aboard a "disco cruise" during the evening of September 4, 1981. At about 11.00p.m. with the event organised by the Hythe Lord Nelson public house football team in full-swing, a man and a woman went overboard off Calshot. With apparent total disregard for his own safety 34 years old Marchwood man Mike Puckett stripped to the waist and plunged into the sea after them. He succeeded in rescuing the woman and whilst fellow passengers and crew got her aboard he went back for the man. His bravery in effecting the rescue was in stark contrast to the foolhardiness of some of his fellow revellers.

The latter half of 1981 was an extremely troublesome priod for the ferry service. A series of decisions and disasters culminated in the cessation of quarter hourly rush hour services on October 17. These included a 15% fare increase on June 1, the introduction of express limited stop bus services by-passing the Hythe terminus in August, the refusal of a subsidy by the Hampshire County Council and the fouling of a propeller on the **Hythe Hotspur** on September 30, necessicitating withdrawal from service for repair leaving only the **Hotspur IV** available with the new vessel still months away from completion.

As the bus company prospered Mr. Tim Morgan was forced to admit,
"Things have not been going well lately . . but we are planning a new approach and we expect to come up with some new ideas to attract people back to the ferry".

As well as the cut back in services, certain redundancies and other measures had to be executed. However by early January 1982, even with delivery of the new vessel still uncertain, things had improved sufficiently for an extra crossing from Hythe at 8.15a.m. to be laid on.

"We think the re-structuring and reorganisation we had to carry out last year," said Mr. Morgan, "is beginning to pay off". He continued, "we are optimistic we have passed our Nadir as far as business is concerned and are looking forward to a prosperous new year".

Fishing from the pier has been a feature of everyday activity through-out it's history but the increase in mindless vandalism over the previous decade forced a decision in December 1981 to limit week-end and holiday fishing by youngsters to organised parties or parental supervision.

Still on the pier, extensive replanking of the pierhead was effected during April and May 1982 necessitating a pedestrian walkway to the southside of the restaurant, an area fenced off for many years previous.

The Summer of 1982 witnessed a mini tourist boom in Southampton and the Waterside area in general. The departures to and triumphal returns from the Falklands of ships like **Canberra** and **Queen Elizabeth II**, and the subsequent **Tall Ships** gathering attracted tourists by the thousands, most of whom wanted to get onto the water by one means or another. The return of these vessels, that of the **Canberra** in particular,

The Canberra returns to Southampton from the Falklands on July 11th 1982 (Reproduced by kind permission of Southern Evening Echo)

saw never to be forgotton emotional scenes.

Even weeks after the euphoria of the returns people clamoured for deckspace on the harbour cruises to see the two leviathans as they underwent overhaul in preparation for their return to civilian duties. One consequence of this unscheduled bounty however was a battle between Southern Coastcrafts and their major competitor, Blue Funnel Ferries, for the extra business. Prices tumbled for each departure until on August 9 hour long cruises were being offered at just 45 pence. Sanity prevailed and by August 12 £1.85 was the going rate for an afternoon excursion.

Vast crowds assembled on the pier on August 25 for the "Parade of Sail" which saw some 70 vessels enter Southampton in procession, the star of which undoubtedly being the Danish full rigged **Danmark**. As the **Hotspur IV** continued to ply the passage, the **Hythe Hotspur** and newly introduced **New Forester** were packed to capacity for this historic and evocative event.

On the previous Saturday (August 21) over 5000 passengers were recorded on the ferry passage alone, breaking all previous records. Such was the interest that persons had to be kept off the pier for half hour periods to enable those already on the ferries to disperse. One unfortunate incident on August 25 saw an eldery woman collapse on the pier but after treatment at Southampton General Hospital Mrs. Sheila Meonsfield was discharged.

Early in March 1983 it was announced that Southern Coastcrafts had won a contract to provide a holiday season cruise programme from Ryde (I.O.W.) pier. The **Hythe Hotspur** was to be employed two or three times weekly at the height of the season. Taking advantage of the positioning of the vessel, her owners were able to offer a mid-week all-day excursion from Hythe Pier to Ryde, which proved very popular.

Firemen were raced along the pier by Land-Rover on August 28, 1983 to extinguish a fire at the very end of the structure. The alarm had been raised by Mrs. Elizabeth Percy who had noticed billowing smoke from her Hotspur House flat.

Being a Sunday, "no boats were operating, otherwise the fire might have been spotted much earlier", Mr. Tim Morgan told the local press. "We believe a cigarette end must have caught between two of the planks and smouldered all morning unnoticed before suddenly flaring up".

Several timbers and iron supports were extensively damaged and firemen remained a considerable time damping down the remaining tinder dry planking.

During 1983 a structural survey was carried out on Hythe Pier by the Netley Marsh based civil engineering company Gifford and Partners. The work involved accurate examination using infra-red apparatus to measure expansion and contraction. Engineer Mr. Malcolm Woolley is on record for saying,
"Nowadays engineers build their structures allowing for movement and expansion, but they don't always get it right . . . The Victorians did not bother about these fine allowances of movement and though the Hythe Pier creaks and groans the structure is able to cope".

The General Estates Company were already actively engaged in efforts to attract grants to help pay for general maintenance of the Pier, which in 1982 alone had cost more than £25,000, when the survey revealed that work costing a quarter of a million pounds would have to be carried out over a five year period.

Unfounded rumours of the pier's imminent closure and subsequent demolition were quickly put down by Mr. Tim Morgan as he explained the requirements of the Gifford survey. Replacement work on parts of the ironwork showing signs of corrosion would have to be implemented with some haste but the supporting piles had been given a clean bill of health. Hampshire County Council had promised £30,000, (actual grants approved with continued support assured have amounted to £65,000 by March 1986), and the New Forest District Council a further £10,000 towards the bill; Southern Coastcrafts having already alloted £60,000. Any fears from commuters that they would have to subsidise the work were also dispelled when the fare increase announced for January 1984 was just 3 pence per single crossing.

Work has subsequently been put into effect and evidence of its continued execution will be a feature of the local landscape during the next couple of years.

A passenger spotted the body of an elderly man floating off the Town Quay on September 17, 1984. Southampton police subsequently retrieved it, announcing no suspicious circumstances.

New Forester

Aerial view of Hythe Marina Village showing proximity to pier.

The later stages of 1984 saw construction work commence on the Hythe Marina project. As this is the most significant change along the Hythe waterfront since the construction of the Pier itself more than a century previous, record should be made herein of the events so far.

During the mid-late sixties material dredged from the site of the Southampton Container Terminal at Millbrook had been deposited into Dibden Bay, thus reclaiming some 800 acres. Having acquired freehold from Associated British Ports, the New Forest District Council offered in May 1981 a brief to developers which included among its many provisos for the 40 acres nearest to Hythe, that the land be used as a marina with facilities for some 500 boats and normal services such as offices, shops, clubhouse, bar and restaurant, boat lifting, sales and storage, etc. Further, a public slipway and access to the waterfront were to be provided along with offsite improvements to access roads.

Several schemes were put before the local authority, with that of Shamrock Developments emerging successfully. Shamrock Developments, whose registered office is in Poole, Dorset but has offices at Southampton's Shamrock Quay proposed to include 225 homes in their scheme to offset high infrastructure costs.

As there is some five metres difference between tidal extremes, it was proposed to keep the water level in the marine basins constant by means of a lock available 24 hours a day, and to provide movement of water in the canals and basins by sluice valves near the "Hythe Marina Village" centre. Each house, built on piled foundations, would have as part of its property a berth, the smallest of which would be 10 metres in length. A "village" centre would include a pub/restaurant, convenience food store, five shops and offices.

The remaining 275 berths, minimum draft 2.5 metres, would be available to yachtsmen for an annual rental.

Extensive negotiations with the New Forest District Council followed before construction work eventually began, by which time a further ten acres had been added to provide an area foi depositing the excavated material in the form of a landscaped hill.

November 1984 saw Sir Christopher Cockerell formally lay the first house brick and following flooding of the first marina basin a month previous, June 1985 saw Chay Blythe perform the offical lock commissioning ceremony. **T.S. Royalist** was the first official craft through the lock, followed by Richard Branson's **Virgin Atlantic Challenger**. The second marina basin was flooded in November 1985, by which time twelve houses were already occupied.

Impression and reality.

The entire area, lock to sluice, including landscaping is expected to be completed by the Summer of 1986. Work on the "village" centre commenced in March 1986 and is expected to last twelve months, with completion of the whole project by 1990.

Just how the development will effect the Hythe ferry and its traffic remains to be seen, but the signs are of a favourable influence.

The ferry services came in for some fierce criticism in December 1985. It was unfortunate that during a cold snap the **New Forester** was out of commission for re-fit and with the **Hythe Hotspur** temporarily laid up because of high running costs, only the aged and slow **Hotspur IV** was available for the passage. Commuter Mrs. Jill Tulip voiced her own opinion in the local newspaper, Forest Reporter, on January 9, 1986. "I am disgusted," she is quoted as saying. "As soon as the cold weather is with us they bring out of mothballs their oldest ferry. Unless you are among the first privileged few who get a seat in the upper salon you are forced to stand packed like sardines, go downstairs below deck where you cannot breathe for smoke, or remain outside on deck and freeze".

Mr. Morgan defending his services and in particular the timing of the refitting of the **New Forester**, replied,
"It has to be done in winter because in summer it is used on tourist cruises which help subsidise the ferry service".

Mr Morgan and Mrs. Tulip did strike accord however when the General Estates Company executive agreed to her request for a ban on smoking on the Hythe Pier train. This move of course also assists with easing the greatest cause of fire risk.

February 28, 1986 saw the retirement of Mr. Tim Morgan. He had been at the forefront of ferry operations since 1969 following his retirement from the local constabulary, detailed in earlier pages. Mr. Morgan's plans for retirement include devoting more time to gardening and fly-fishing. Although he and his wife intend to travel more, they will continue to live in Hythe and will no doubt continue an interest in the activities of the passage.

Replacing Mr. Morgan will be Mr. Gerald Case, a former ship repair yard and marina manager, who will take up his post by June 1986.

Mr. Morgan is relinquishing his position at a time when the future of ferry operations would appear more sound than in recent times, and with Mr. Michael Percy expressing an optimism and confidence that goes with 99 years of family involvement on the Hythe-Southampton Ferry.

Mr. Tim Morgan.

Ferry Boats

This section includes extracts from an article entitled "A Tribute to the Hythe Ferry" first published in **Sea Breezes** in September 1974 and reproduced by permission of the editor.

Emerald

On March 10, 1830 the "new steam boat" **Emerald** inaugurated the first steamer service to Hythe.

The 31 ton wooden paddler **Emerald** which had been built by John Rubie of Cross House, Southampton and launched late in 1829 was 68 ft. in length, 10 ft. in breadth, 7 ft. in depth and propelled by a 10 h.p. engine.

By June 1832, it would appear that the **Emerald** had relinquished the Hythe service to concentrate on her Isle of Wight commitments.

Forester

Day, Summers and Company, built the **Forester** at Millbrook in 1836 after having announced in June of the previous year that an iron paddle boat was under construction for the Hythe—Southampton ferry. They offered the vessel for sale on completion as the profession of steam boat proprietor was not in accordance with their business. The buyers, Capt J.H. Knight, senior, and Smith and Company, were able to boast of being the owners of the first non-wooden steam boat built South of the Thames. She was 65 ft. 5 ins. in length, 10 ft. in breadth, 5 ft. 11 ins. in depth and propelled by a 6 h.p. engine, built by Boulton and Watt.

Gipsy

The third Hythe steamer, the **Gipsy**, entered service on August 25, 1845.

The **Gipsy** had been built by Summers, Day and Baldock, of Northam, and launched on July 5. Miss Emily Clarke, daughter of one of her proprietors, performed the christening before she made her proving trip to the Beaulieu River on August 20.

Popularly described as being a "light and elegant steamer" she was of 20.5 tons register with her dimensions being 73 ft. 10 ins. x 11 ft. 1 in. x 5 ft. 1 in. Her paddles were turned by a 16 h.p. engine. A 14 in. draft allowed her to advance further up Hythe hard than either the **Emerald** or the **Forester**.

The **Gipsy's** owners suspended operations in December 11, 1847.

Prince Alfred

The next vessel to arrive on the ferry was the former Thames steamer **Prince Alfred**, shortly after the registration of the Hythe and Southampton Steam Ferry Company on July 7, 1855.

The **Prince Alfred** had been built by G. Chitham of Frindsbury, Kent in 1846 and registered at Rochester (official number 9449) her registration not being transferred to Southampton until her sale to E.N. Harvey, of Fawley on January 29, 1857.

It is thought that the **Prince Alfred** contributed to her owner's downfall by being "old and troublesome." Often Southampton-bound passengers had to wait for the crew to turn her around by means of long poles, in preparation for the next journey.

Constructed of wood, she was of 19 tons net, 30 gross, 70 ft. 4 in. in length, 11 ft. 7 in. in breadth, 5 ft. 4 in. in depth and had her paddles turned by a 20 h.p. engine. She ended her career when sold to W. Winckworth, of Hythe, on September 12, 1861 as a wreck for breaking up.

Lady Elizabeth

The **Lady Elizabeth**, built of iron and propelled by a 28. h.p. engine, weighed in at 37 net tons, 59 gross. She was 98 ft. 4 in. long, 13 ft. 11 in. wide and 6 ft. 6 in. in depth. It was found that she was too big for the service, so on July 15, 1858 she was sold by a Mr. Greaves, who received £100 commission for his efforts, to E. Dorling, of Ipswich.

The registration (official no. 18151), was subsequently transferred on August 2 to Mr. Dorling's home port, where the still very young paddler was to serve until 1871. However her ownership changed hands twice more while in this port — to the Waterman Steam Packet Company, of London, in 1868 and to T.C. Jennings, of Ipswich a year later.

In 1871, she passed into the possession of one Anthony Bannister, of Hull who took her to her third port of registration. In 1875 she became the property of William Fisher West; in 1876 — Michael Wrangles Clarke and in 1890 — the Goole and Hull Steam Packet Company; serving all from the port of her registration. She disappeared from the register in 1901.

Louisa

In fact, the 23-net ton **Louisa's** gross tonnage was only equal to the net of her predecessor. Built by J.Hodgkinson, of Cross House, Southampton, the **Louisa** (official no. 22538) was constructed of iron, 79 ft. 8 in. in length 12 ft. 4 in. in breadth and 5 ft. 6 in. in depth.

A 20 h.p. engine turned her paddles and in favourable conditions she could make seven knots. This vessel served her owners well until their liquidation when she was sold on September 21, 1861 to W. Winckworth, who subsequently operated the service.

In 1864 as many as 271 passengers were permitted to be carried at any one time, but by 1889 this number had been reduced by the Board of Trade to 150. The safety regulations ordered by the Board enforced the provision of lifebouys to be doubled to four, with the retention of the original 50 lifejackets despite the decrease in passengers. Even with the new limits, the **Louisa** appeared overcrowded, hence crossings were more popular in a half-filled boat.

She ended her days as a ballast barge upon entry into service of the **Hotspur**. Her registration was cancelled on June 12, 1893 following her demolition.

Frederica

Day, Summers and Company built the **Frederica** (official number 44904) in 1863, to the order of W. Winckworth and R. Barns, also of Hythe. This vessel was to be very popular, a trifle smaller — 21 net tons, 35 gross — than the **Louisa** and of less passenger capacity — 230 in 1863. She was 80 ft. 4 in. long, 12 ft. 1 in. wide, 5 ft. 6 in. in depth and powered by a 12 h.p. engine.

On January 22, 1868 W. Winckworth acquired sole ownership and operated her alongside the **Louisa** until together they passed into the hands of F. Fry, of Hythe on May 24, 1872.

With the **Louisa**, the **Frederica** was purchased by Mr. James Percy on March 2, 1887 and, again like the **Louisa** ended her days as a barge. Her register was closed on August 5, 1897.

Princess

This 6 h.p. screw steamer operated for a short while in 1871. Owned by Slade & Tiller of Southampton, the **Princess** was 37 ft. long, built to carry 36 passengers and according to a contemporary press report was "fitted up with all the latest improvements, both in her machinery department and also in her cabin and other accommodation, carrying side and masthead lights, screens, steam whistle, life-buoys, anchor and cable and all the necessaries required by the Board of Trade."

Netley

A 9 ton screw steamer, the **Netley** was placed on a station between Netley and Southampton with calls at Cracknorehard and Hythe Pier by her owner, William Gannaway on July 1, 1882. She was licenced to carry 60 passengers and propelled by a 10 h.p. engine.

Hotspur

Designed by Hythe naval architect C.P. Clayton, the **Hotspur**, official number 94514, was 80 ft. in length, 15 ft. in breadth and had a depth of 6 ft.

Her paddles were turned by a 25 h.p. oscillating cylinder steam engine, probably one of the last of that type, capable of moving the vessel at a speed of about 8 knots. Her registered tonnage was 39 net, 62 gross and she was built to carry 200 passengers.

She was sold on January 1, 1915 to the General Estates Co. Ltd. Renamed **G.E.C.** and after having her machinery and fittings removed, her hulk was taken to Dibden Bay where it eventually rusted away. The registration was cancelled on May 12, 1930.

Hampton

Mr. Percy's second new vessel was ready for operation in May 1894. The 33 net, 63 gross ton **Hampton** (official number 104035) had been built, like the **Lady Elizabeth** and **Louisa**, by Day, Summers and Company. She was 80 ft. long, 16 ft. 1 in. wide at deck (25 ft. over sponsons) and 5 ft. 8 in. in depth.

Fitted with a 25h.p. compound, inclined, surface condensing paddle engine with cylinders of 14 and 24in. diameter, 27 in. stroke, her boiler was 8 ft. in diameter and 7 ft. 8 in. long, designed for working pressure of 80 lbs.

Her design allowed for a sunk deckhouse at each end, one each for first and second-class passengers, with a promenade deck well endowed with seating above the first-class deckhouse. There were also seats all around the deck. Certified to carry 214 passengers, she was able to achieve speeds of 10½ knots and cost her owner over £2,000. The lighting of this iron constructed vessel was by paraffin and it was not until shortly prior to the First World War that it was converted, along with that of the **Hotspur**, to electricity.

Her register was closed on November 27, 1936 following her disposal through brokers to a Dutch firm of shipbreakers, who had her towed to Rotterdam for demolition. Her fate however was not too clear as there have been stories of her working on the Dutch canals during the Second World War.

Hamble

Introduced in October 1915, by the General Estates Company, the 40 ft. motor launch **Hamble** was used in conjunction with or in the place of the **Hotspur** and/or **Hampton**. She was able to carry 50-60 passengers.

Southtown

Built in 1896 for the Yarmouth and Gorleston Steamboat Company, her dimensions were 91 ft. x 16 ft. (depth unknown) and tonnages, 33 net, 72 gross. A screw steamer, the **Southtown** was able to carry 300 passengers and was driven by a 30 h.p. engine.

Her career ended with 19 years of pleasure cruising along the Norfolk coast before disposal to Dutch shipbreakers in 1965.

It is not certain just how much time was spent on the Hythe passage although evidence of her arrival on September 29, 1918 is available.

Yarmouth

The dimensions of the **Yarmouth**, built in 1895 to the order of the Yarmouth & Gorleston Steamboat Company, were 74 ft. x 16 ft. x 7 ft. 9 ins. and tonnages 25 net, 56 gross. Able to carry about 180 passengers this screw steamer was driven by a 14 h.p. engine. After 23 years of pleasure cruising along the Norfolk Coast, following ferry duties, she was sold privately in Great Yarmouth in 1969 before eventually being preserved in London's St. Katherine's Yacht Haven Maritime Museum during 1976. Like the **Southtown** the duration of her stay on these waters is not certain, but is believed to have been between November/December 1918 and January 1921.

Hotspur

The launching of the second **Hotspur** took place at the East Cowes yard of John Samuel White and Company on January 17, 1927.

The new **Hotspur** was 80 ft. long, 18 ft. wide with a moulded depth of 6 ft. 3 in. She was a twin-screw motorship propelled by one Vickers Petter 140 b.h.p. 4-cylinder, reversible type, heavy-oil engine arranged to drive a propellor at either end of the vessel and move her at speeds of up to 10½ knots.

She also had a Vickers Petter auxiliary set, coupled to an air compressor, the function of which was to supply starting air to the main engine and for driving the electric generator and general service pump.

Her builders were also her designers and their ideas resulted in a fine flush-deck vessel with upright bow and stern. There was a rudder at each end of a hull with five watertight compartments — fore-peak, fore-cabin, motor room, store and after-peak. Her upperworks comprised a deckhouse on the landing deck above the fore-cabin, a deckhouse aft and a wheelhouse above the motor room.

The **Hotspur**, certified to carry 300 passengers, was the first vessel on the ferry to be electrically lighted from the outset. Tonnages were 24 net and 56 gross. Her official registration number was 149286.

When the **Hotspur IV** was commissioned in 1947, the ageing **Hotspur** was transferred to the Yarmouth and Gorleston Steamboat Company. Now a steamer, folowing conversion by Elliott and Garwood, of Lowestoft in 1932, she served this concern until 1961 when she was sold to the Yardarm Club of London. Work of converting her into a restaurant was completed in 1963, when she was renamed **Yard Arm Club**, although the register retained her original name.

Moored on the North Bank of the Thames between the Hungerford and Waterloo bridges, the **Yard Arm Club** was a joint project of the Kengore Hotels and Watermen Caterers Ltd. In 1966 her ownership passed into the hands of the Yard Arm Club Ltd., whose proposed change of name to **Emma Hamilton** did not materialise, although it is possible she sported this name on her bow. Her name, however, was changed a year later to **Hispaniola**, a name which she retained until her removal from the aforementioned site during the mid seventies.

Hotspur II

The **Hotspur II** (official number 165079, Rowhedge Yard No. S.529), is of 32 tons net, 54 gross, 56 ft. 5 in. long, 17 ft. wide and 6 ft. 2 in. in depth. Covered accommodation was provided in the shape of an upper and a lower cabin for about a third of her certified limit of 300 passengers. Seats, some doubling as life-buoys, were provided on the deck and above the upper cabin, where the wheelhouse was situated. Under normal conditions this area was reserved for crew only.

The motor room was to the rear of the lower cabin, entrance being obtained via the motor room cover aft of the upper cabin. The funnel was situated between the upper cabin and motor room cover behind the wheelhouse. Her builders provided her with two 4-cylinder Atlantic oil engines capable of moving the vessel at a speed of $8\frac{1}{2}$knots.

The **Hotspur II** served the passage from 1936 until 1978 before being sold to a River Clyde ferry concern who renamed her **Kenilworth**.

Carrick Lass

The **Carrick Lass**, official number 164030, had been built by H. McLean and Sons Ltd. of Govan in 1934 to the order of R. L. Greig. Constructed of wood, she was of 16 tons net, 38 gross, 57 ft. 6 in. in length, 16 ft. in breath and 7 ft. 4 in. in depth. Her propelling machinery comprised of 2 x 60 h.p. Gleniffer oil engines.

The **Carrick Lass**, taken over by the Admiralty in 1940, met with a watery grave as the ship transporting her to West Africa was sunk.

Hotspur III

The **Hotspur III** was of the same design as the **Hotspur II** but slightly larger, the dimensional differences being, net tonnage 34, gross tonnage 55, length 56 ft. 6 in., passenger capacity 304 with her official number being 165127 (Rowhedge Yard No. S.555)

During 1949 the **Hotspur II** and **Hotspur III** were each re-engined with two 4-cylinder Gardner engines, as fitted in the **Hotspur IV**. The **Hotspur III** was re-engined in 1969, this time with two 6-cylinder Kelvin engines.

She was broken up early in 1981.

Hotspur IV

After the war an order was placed, again with the Rowhedge Ironworks Co. Ltd., for a third vessel of the design afforded to the **Hotspur II** and **Hotspur III**. The **Hotspur IV**, the oldest of the present fleet, is however, rather larger. Her dimensions are 64 ft. x 19 ft. 2 in. x 6 ft. 4 in. with a net tonnage of 23 and gross of 54. She was fitted with two 4-cylinder 65 i.h.p. Gardner oil engines, capable of moving her at $8\frac{1}{2}$ knots and is licensed to carry 350 passengers. Her official registration number is 167903 and Rowhedge yard number is S.673.

The speed of the **Hotspur IV** was increased to $9\frac{1}{2}$ knots with the added power of two new 4-cylinder Kelvin engines in 1968 and her appearance improved when her funnel was replaced by slender twin uptakes.

Hythe Hotspur

Built in Sussex as the **Southsea Queen**, she was purchased by General Estates Company in June 1978. Renamed **Hythe Hotspur** in September 1978 this vessel is 80 feet in length, has a draught of 5 ft. 8 in. and a gross tonnage of 119. Her official number is 362708 and she is certified to carry 250 passengers (245 in winter) with a crew of 9.

Princessa

Built in 1921 the **Princessa** measures 71 ft. x 18 ft. and weighs in at 49 tons gross. She has a passenger capacity of 170 and is owned by the Blue Funnel Steamers Ltd. She is occasionally chartered by the hour for the passage.

New Forester

After numerous problems the **New Forester** entered service on August 20, 1982. Built by the Arun Yacht and Boat Company of Littlehampton the **New Forester** had been launched by trolley from the quayside down a slipway into a small yacht basin open to the River Arun without ceremony on March 17, 1982.

She measures up 66 feet in length, 21 feet in width and has a maximum draught of 4 feet 6 ins, with a tonnage of 49 gross. Her twin screws are powered by the two Kelvin 6 cylinder diesel engines of 1971 vintage that once powered the **Hotspur III**.

The **New Forester** is certified to carry 150 passengers with a crew of 3 on the passage or 110 passengers with a crew of 5 on excursion work between limits at Bembridge (I.O.W.) and the Needles, at a service speed of 8 knots. Her official number is 700270.

THE AUTHOR

Alan Titheridge lives locally with his wife and daughter. He is a buyer, by profession, employed by the Millbrook Electric Appliance Manufacturers, Dimplex Heating Limited.

As well as a keen interest in local history, particularly that relating to Hythe village, 35 years old Alan enjoys Squash, playing his sport with the Applemore Squash Racquets Club.

Travelling is also of particular interest with Australia being the author's favourite country.

When time allows, he also likes to relax with a good book and includes among his favourite authors Ronnie Delderfield and Thomas Hardy.

This is the second edition of Alan's first publication and he has also written numerous articles and letters for an assortment of shipping magazines.

Hotspur III arriving at Town Quay.